Dear Future Exam Success Story

First of all, **THANK YOU** for purchasing Mometrix study materials!

Second, congratulations! You are one of the few determined test-takers who are committed to doing whatever it takes to excel on your exam. **You have come to the right place.** We developed these study materials with one goal in mind: to deliver you the information you need in a format that's concise and easy to use.

In addition to optimizing your guide for the content of the test, we've outlined our recommended steps for breaking down the preparation process into small, attainable goals so you can make sure you stay on track.

We've also analyzed the entire test-taking process, identifying the most common pitfalls and showing how you can overcome them and be ready for any curveball the test throws you.

Standardized testing is one of the biggest obstacles on your road to success, which only increases the importance of doing well in the high-pressure, high-stakes environment of test day. Your results on this test could have a significant impact on your future, and this guide provides the information and practical advice to help you achieve your full potential on test day.

Your success is our success

We would love to hear from you! If you would like to share the story of your exam success or if you have any questions or comments in regard to our products, please contact us at **800-673-8175** or **support@mometrix.com**.

Thanks again for your business and we wish you continued success!

Sincerely,
The Mometrix Test Preparation Team

Written and edited by the Mometrix Exam Secrets Test Prep Team
Printed in the United States of America

TABLE OF CONTENTS

INTRODUCTION 1
STRATEGY #1 – PLAN BIG, STUDY SMALL 2
STRATEGY #2 – MAKE YOUR STUDYING COUNT 3
STRATEGY #3 – PRACTICE THE RIGHT WAY 4
TEST-TAKING STRATEGIES 5
READING 9
- VOCABULARY 9
- COMPREHENSION SKILLS 15
- RESPONSE SKILLS 21
- LITERARY ELEMENTS 24
- LITERARY GENRES 32
- AUTHOR'S PURPOSE AND CRAFT 41

WRITING 53
- WRITING PROCESS 53
- ESSAY STRUCTURE AND ORGANIZATION 56
- GRAMMAR 60
- EXTENDED CONSTRUCTED RESPONSE 94
- INFORMATIONAL TEXT EXAMPLE 99

PRACTICE TEST #1 107
- READING 107
- EXTENDED RESPONSE 116
- REVISING 118
- EDITING 122

ANSWER KEY AND EXPLANATIONS FOR TEST #1 124
- READING 124
- EXTENDED RESPONSE 129
- REVISING 130
- EDITING 132

PRACTICE TEST #2 135
- READING 135
- EXTENDED RESPONSE 146
- REVISING 148
- EDITING 152

ANSWER KEY AND EXPLANATIONS FOR TEST #2 155
- READING 155
- EXTENDED RESPONSE 159
- REVISING 160
- EDITING 162

PRACTICE TEST #3 165

HOW TO OVERCOME TEST ANXIETY — 166
ONLINE RESOURCES — 172

Introduction

Thank you for purchasing this resource! You have made the choice to prepare yourself for a test that could have a huge impact on your future, and this guide is designed to help you be fully ready for test day. Obviously, it's important to have a solid understanding of the test material, but you also need to be prepared for the unique environment and stressors of the test, so that you can perform to the best of your abilities.

For this purpose, the first section that appears in this guide is the **Success Strategies**. We've devoted countless hours to meticulously researching what works and what doesn't, and we've boiled down our findings to the four most impactful steps you can take to improve your performance on the test. We start at the beginning with study planning and move through the preparation process, all the way to the testing strategies that will help you get the most out of what you know when you're finally sitting in front of the test.

We recommend that you start preparing for your test as far in advance as possible. However, if you've bought this guide as a last-minute study resource and only have a few days before your test, we recommend that you skip over the first two Success Strategies since they address a long-term study plan.

If you struggle with **test anxiety**, we strongly encourage you to check out our recommendations for how you can overcome it. Test anxiety is a formidable foe, but it can be beaten, and we want to make sure you have the tools you need to defeat it.

Strategy #1 – Plan Big, Study Small

There's a lot riding on your performance. If you want to ace this test, you're going to need to keep your skills sharp and the material fresh in your mind. You need a plan that lets you review everything you need to know while still fitting in your schedule. We'll break this strategy down into three categories.

Information Organization

Start with the information you already have: the official test outline. From this, you can make a complete list of all the concepts you need to cover before the test. Organize these concepts into groups that can be studied together, and create a list of any related vocabulary you need to learn so you can brush up on any difficult terms. You'll want to keep this vocabulary list handy once you actually start studying since you may need to add to it along the way.

Time Management

Once you have your set of study concepts, decide how to spread them out over the time you have left before the test. Break your study plan into small, clear goals so you have a manageable task for each day and know exactly what you're doing. Then just focus on one small step at a time. When you manage your time this way, you don't need to spend hours at a time studying. Studying a small block of content for a short period each day helps you retain information better and avoid stressing over how much you have left to do. You can relax knowing that you have a plan to cover everything in time. In order for this strategy to be effective though, you have to start studying early and stick to your schedule. Avoid the exhaustion and futility that comes from last-minute cramming!

Study Environment

The environment you study in has a big impact on your learning. Studying in a coffee shop, while probably more enjoyable, is not likely to be as fruitful as studying in a quiet room. It's important to keep distractions to a minimum. You're only planning to study for a short block of time, so make the most of it. Don't pause to check your phone or get up to find a snack. It's also important to **avoid multitasking**. Research has consistently shown that multitasking will make your studying dramatically less effective. Your study area should also be comfortable and well-lit so you don't have the distraction of straining your eyes or sitting on an uncomfortable chair.

The time of day you study is also important. You want to be rested and alert. Don't wait until just before bedtime. Study when you'll be most likely to comprehend and remember. Even better, if you know what time of day your test will be, set that time aside for study. That way your brain will be used to working on that subject at that specific time and you'll have a better chance of recalling information.

Finally, it can be helpful to team up with others who are studying for the same test. Your actual studying should be done in as isolated an environment as possible, but the work of organizing the information and setting up the study plan can be divided up. In between study sessions, you can discuss with your teammates the concepts that you're all studying and quiz each other on the details. Just be sure that your teammates are as serious about the test as you are. If you find that your study time is being replaced with social time, you might need to find a new team.

Strategy #2 – Make Your Studying Count

You're devoting a lot of time and effort to preparing for this test, so you want to be absolutely certain it will pay off. This means doing more than just reading the content and hoping you can remember it on test day. It's important to make every minute of study count. There are two main areas you can focus on to make your studying count.

Retention

It doesn't matter how much time you study if you can't remember the material. You need to make sure you are retaining the concepts. To check your retention of the information you're learning, try recalling it at later times with minimal prompting. Try carrying around flashcards and glance at one or two from time to time or ask a friend who's also studying for the test to quiz you.

To enhance your retention, look for ways to put the information into practice so that you can apply it rather than simply recalling it. If you're using the information in practical ways, it will be much easier to remember. Similarly, it helps to solidify a concept in your mind if you're not only reading it to yourself but also explaining it to someone else. Ask a friend to let you teach them about a concept you're a little shaky on (or speak aloud to an imaginary audience if necessary). As you try to summarize, define, give examples, and answer your friend's questions, you'll understand the concepts better and they will stay with you longer. Finally, step back for a big picture view and ask yourself how each piece of information fits with the whole subject. When you link the different concepts together and see them working together as a whole, it's easier to remember the individual components.

Finally, practice showing your work on any multi-step problems, even if you're just studying. Writing out each step you take to solve a problem will help solidify the process in your mind, and you'll be more likely to remember it during the test.

Modality

Modality simply refers to the means or method by which you study. Choosing a study modality that fits your own individual learning style is crucial. No two people learn best in exactly the same way, so it's important to know your strengths and use them to your advantage.

For example, if you learn best by visualization, focus on visualizing a concept in your mind and draw an image or a diagram. Try color-coding your notes, illustrating them, or creating symbols that will trigger your mind to recall a learned concept. If you learn best by hearing or discussing information, find a study partner who learns the same way or read aloud to yourself. Think about how to put the information in your own words. Imagine that you are giving a lecture on the topic and record yourself so you can listen to it later.

For any learning style, flashcards can be helpful. Organize the information so you can take advantage of spare moments to review. Underline key words or phrases. Use different colors for different categories. Mnemonic devices (such as creating a short list in which every item starts with the same letter) can also help with retention. Find what works best for you and use it to store the information in your mind most effectively and easily.

Strategy #3 – Practice the Right Way

Your success on test day depends not only on how many hours you put into preparing, but also on whether you prepared the right way. It's good to check along the way to see if your studying is paying off. One of the most effective ways to do this is by taking practice tests to evaluate your progress. Practice tests are useful because they show exactly where you need to improve. Every time you take a practice test, pay special attention to these three groups of questions:

- The questions you got wrong
- The questions you had to guess on, even if you guessed right
- The questions you found difficult or slow to work through

This will show you exactly what your weak areas are, and where you need to devote more study time. Ask yourself why each of these questions gave you trouble. Was it because you didn't understand the material? Was it because you didn't remember the vocabulary? Do you need more repetitions on this type of question to build speed and confidence? Dig into those questions and figure out how you can strengthen your weak areas as you go back to review the material.

Additionally, many practice tests have a section explaining the answer choices. It can be tempting to read the explanation and think that you now have a good understanding of the concept. However, an explanation likely only covers part of the question's broader context. Even if the explanation makes perfect sense, **go back and investigate** every concept related to the question until you're positive you have a thorough understanding.

As you go along, keep in mind that the practice test is just that: practice. Memorizing these questions and answers will not be very helpful on the actual test because it is unlikely to have any of the same exact questions. If you only know the right answers to the sample questions, you won't be prepared for the real thing. **Study the concepts** until you understand them fully, and then you'll be able to answer any question that shows up on the test.

It's important to wait on the practice tests until you're ready. If you take a test on your first day of study, you may be overwhelmed by the amount of material covered and how much you need to learn. Work up to it gradually.

On test day, you'll need to be prepared for answering questions, managing your time, and using the test-taking strategies you've learned. It's a lot to balance, like a mental marathon that will have a big impact on your future. Like training for a marathon, you'll need to start slowly and work your way up. When test day arrives, you'll be ready.

Start with the strategies you've read in the first two Success Strategies—plan your course and study in the way that works best for you. If you have time, consider using multiple study resources to get different approaches to the same concepts. It can be helpful to see difficult concepts from more than one angle. Then find a good source for practice tests. Many times, the test website will suggest potential study resources or provide sample tests.

Test-Taking Strategies

This section contains a list of test-taking strategies that you may find helpful as you work through the test. By taking what you know and applying logical thought, you can maximize your chances of answering any question correctly!

It is very important to realize that every question is different and every person is different: no single strategy will work on every question, and no single strategy will work for every person. That's why we've included all of them here, so you can try them out and determine which ones work best for different types of questions and which ones work best for you.

Question Strategies

✓ Read Carefully

Read the question and the answer choices carefully. Don't miss the question because you misread the terms. You have plenty of time to read each question thoroughly and make sure you understand what is being asked. Yet a happy medium must be attained, so don't waste too much time. You must read carefully and efficiently.

✓ Contextual Clues

Look for contextual clues. If the question includes a word you are not familiar with, look at the immediate context for some indication of what the word might mean. Contextual clues can often give you all the information you need to decipher the meaning of an unfamiliar word. Even if you can't determine the meaning, you may be able to narrow down the possibilities enough to make a solid guess at the answer to the question.

✓ Prefixes

If you're having trouble with a word in the question or answer choices, try dissecting it. Take advantage of every clue that the word might include. Prefixes can be a huge help. Usually, they allow you to determine a basic meaning. *Pre-* means before, *post-* means after, *pro-* is positive, *de-* is negative. From prefixes, you can get an idea of the general meaning of the word and try to put it into context.

✓ Hedge Words

Watch out for critical hedge words, such as *likely, may, can, often, almost, mostly, usually, generally, rarely*, and *sometimes*. Question writers insert these hedge phrases to cover every possibility. Often an answer choice will be wrong simply because it leaves no room for exception. Be on guard for answer choices that have definitive words such as *exactly* and *always*.

✓ Switchback Words

Stay alert for *switchbacks*. These are the words and phrases frequently used to alert you to shifts in thought. The most common switchback words are *but, although*, and *however*. Others include *nevertheless, on the other hand, even though, while, in spite of, despite*, and *regardless of*. Switchback words are important to catch because they can change the direction of the question or an answer choice.

✓ Face Value

When in doubt, use common sense. Accept the situation in the problem at face value. Don't read too much into it. These problems will not require you to make wild assumptions. If you have to go beyond creativity and warp time or space in order to have an answer choice fit the question, then you should move on and consider the other answer choices. These are normal problems rooted in reality. The applicable relationship or explanation may not be readily apparent, but it is there for you to figure out. Use your common sense to interpret anything that isn't clear.

Answer Choice Strategies

✓ Answer Selection

The most thorough way to pick an answer choice is to identify and eliminate wrong answers until only one is left, then confirm it is the correct answer. Sometimes an answer choice may immediately seem right, but be careful. The test writers will usually put more than one reasonable answer choice on each question, so take a second to read all of them and make sure that the other choices are not equally obvious. As long as you have time left, it is better to read every answer choice than to pick the first one that looks right without checking the others.

✓ Answer Choice Families

An answer choice family consists of two (in rare cases, three) answer choices that are very similar in construction and cannot all be true at the same time. If you see two answer choices that are direct opposites or parallels, one of them is usually the correct answer. For instance, if one answer choice says that quantity *x* increases and another either says that quantity *x* decreases (opposite) or says that quantity *y* increases (parallel), then those answer choices would fall into the same family. An answer choice that doesn't match the construction of the answer choice family is more likely to be incorrect. Most questions will not have answer choice families, but when they do appear, you should be prepared to recognize them.

✓ Eliminate Answers

Eliminate answer choices as soon as you realize they are wrong, but make sure you consider all possibilities. If you are eliminating answer choices and realize that the last one you are left with is also wrong, don't panic. Start over and consider each choice again. There may be something you missed the first time that you will realize on the second pass.

✓ Avoid Fact Traps

Don't be distracted by an answer choice that is factually true but doesn't answer the question. You are looking for the choice that answers the question. Stay focused on what the question is asking for so you don't accidentally pick an answer that is true but incorrect. Always go back to the question and make sure the answer choice you've selected actually answers the question and is not merely a true statement.

✓ Extreme Statements

In general, you should avoid answers that put forth extreme actions as standard practice or proclaim controversial ideas as established fact. An answer choice that states the "process should be used in certain situations, if..." is much more likely to be correct than one that states the "process should be discontinued completely." The first is a calm rational statement and doesn't even make a definitive, uncompromising stance, using a hedge word *if* to provide wiggle room, whereas the second choice is far more extreme.

⊘ BENCHMARK

As you read through the answer choices and you come across one that seems to answer the question well, mentally select that answer choice. This is not your final answer, but it's the one that will help you evaluate the other answer choices. The one that you selected is your benchmark or standard for judging each of the other answer choices. Every other answer choice must be compared to your benchmark. That choice is correct until proven otherwise by another answer choice beating it. If you find a better answer, then that one becomes your new benchmark. Once you've decided that no other choice answers the question as well as your benchmark, you have your final answer.

⊘ PREDICT THE ANSWER

Before you even start looking at the answer choices, it is often best to try to predict the answer. When you come up with the answer on your own, it is easier to avoid distractions and traps because you will know exactly what to look for. The right answer choice is unlikely to be word-for-word what you came up with, but it should be a close match. Even if you are confident that you have the right answer, you should still take the time to read each option before moving on.

General Strategies

⊘ TOUGH QUESTIONS

If you are stumped on a problem or it appears too hard or too difficult, don't waste time. Move on! Remember though, if you can quickly check for obviously incorrect answer choices, your chances of guessing correctly are greatly improved. Before you completely give up, at least try to knock out a couple of possible answers. Eliminate what you can and then guess at the remaining answer choices before moving on.

⊘ CHECK YOUR WORK

Since you will probably not know every term listed and the answer to every question, it is important that you get credit for the ones that you do know. Don't miss any questions through careless mistakes. If at all possible, try to take a second to look back over your answer selection and make sure you've selected the correct answer choice and haven't made a costly careless mistake (such as marking an answer choice that you didn't mean to mark). This quick double check should more than pay for itself in caught mistakes for the time it costs.

⊘ DON'T RUSH

It is very easy to make errors when you are in a hurry. Maintaining a fast pace in answering questions is pointless if it makes you miss questions that you would have gotten right otherwise. Test writers like to include distracting information and wrong answers that seem right. Taking a little extra time to avoid careless mistakes can make all the difference in your test score. Find a pace that allows you to be confident in the answers that you select.

⊘ KEEP MOVING

Panicking will not help you pass the test, so do your best to stay calm and keep moving. Taking deep breaths and going through the answer elimination steps you practiced can help to break through a stress barrier and keep your pace.

Final Notes

The combination of a solid foundation of content knowledge and the confidence that comes from practicing your plan for applying that knowledge is the key to maximizing your performance on test day. As your foundation of content knowledge is built up and strengthened, you'll find that the strategies included in this chapter become more and more effective in helping you quickly sift through the distractions and traps of the test to isolate the correct answer.

Now that you're preparing to move forward into the test content chapters of this book, be sure to keep your goal in mind. As you read, think about how you will be able to apply this information on the test. If you've already seen sample questions for the test and you have an idea of the question format and style, try to come up with questions of your own that you can answer based on what you're reading. This will give you valuable practice applying your knowledge in the same ways you can expect to on test day.

Good luck and good studying!

Reading

Vocabulary

Dictionary

A print or digital dictionary can be used to find out many things about a word. A dictionary will show the correct pronunciation of a word, provide its meaning, and identify what part of speech the word is. It will also tell how the word was derived—that is, what words it came from originally. A dictionary will have a **pronunciation guide** for each word that shows how to sound it out and where its syllables start and end. It will use symbols to indicate sounds, and will also use sample sounds (the "a" in "bad," for instance). A dictionary lists all of the meanings of a word and the parts of speech the word can be used as.

> **example** \ ig-'zam-pəl\ noun
> 1. something that shows what a group of things is like
> 2. a model that should be either copied or avoided
> 3. a punishment meant to serve as a warning to others

Example:

Julia used her dictionary to check the various meanings of the word *clear*. She found this entry:

> **clear** (klîr) adjective
> 1. obvious.
> 2. easily seen through
> 3. free from flaw or blemish
> 4. free from guilt; untroubled
> 5. out of the way
> 6. to tidy *v*
> 7. to free *v*
> 8. to earn *v*

Identify which definition of *clear* is used in the following sentence:

Janet stood *clear* of the crowd pushing to get through the door.

The correct answer is meaning 5: "out of the way." If you substitute that definition for the word, the sentence makes sense. Meanings 1, 2, 3, and 4 do not fit with the context of the sentence. Meanings 6, 7, and 8 are verbs and "clear" as it is used in the sample is an adjective. When considering which meaning is being used, always check for context clues in the sentence or in the sentences before or after the sentence in which the word is used. Dictionaries also tell you how to pronounce words and often the derivation of the word, although that is not given here.

Thesaurus

A **thesaurus** is a reference book that gives **synonyms** of words. It is different from a dictionary because a thesaurus does not give definitions. A thesaurus can be helpful in finding the meaning of an unfamiliar word when reading. If the meaning of a synonym is known, then the meaning of the unfamiliar word will be known. Another time in which a thesaurus can be helpful is when writing. Using a thesaurus helps authors to vary their word choice.

Glossary

A **glossary** is a **list of terms and their definitions** that can be found **at the back** of certain types of books, such as textbooks or reference books. A glossary does not have the definitions of all words, like a dictionary, but instead gives the definitions of the important terms within that particular book which are either uncommon or newly introduced. One may use a glossary when reading a book about economics or a chapter in a science textbook, for example, to define some of the technical terms within the text.

Denotative and Connotative Meanings

The **denotative meaning** of a word is the exact dictionary definition of the word. The **connotative meaning** of a word is the emotion conveyed by the use of the word in context. The word may have associated meaning in addition to its dictionary definition. For example, the word *home* is defined in the dictionary as a place where a person or people live. When a reader sees the word in the following context: "Marisol walked briskly *home*, where the smell of fresh-baked apple pie wafted through the warm kitchen," the reader will associate the meaning of the word with coziness and a feeling of well-being. The connotative meaning of a word in a passage can be found by looking at the context clues.

Example

Determine the connotative meaning of the word *ancient* in the following sentence.

> Amy pulled an *ancient* calculator out of the desk, and sat down to figure out how to use it.

In the example, the word 'ancient' literally means very old. The connotative meaning of the word ancient suggests that the calculator does not work as well as more modern versions. in technology, ancient is relative to what is currently being used. For example, a computer may be out of date in a couple years, whereas an ancient society may date back several thousand years.

Using Context to Determine the Meanings of Words

Readers of all levels will encounter words that they have either never seen or that they have seen before but still don't know what it means. The best way to define a word in **context** is to look for nearby words that can assist in learning the meaning of the word.

Context Clues

Context clues are hints about the meaning of a word. They are the words or phrases in the sentence or sentences before and after a new or unfamiliar word. **Context clues** give the reader an idea about what a word means. A context clue may also contain words that help define the new word or an example of what the new word means. A context clue in the form of an example may contain the words including 'such as', a dash, or a colon before stated information.

Using context clues to figure out meaning can be helpful when learning a new set of vocabulary words or reading a difficult text. The dictionary definition of a word can always be looked up to double-check intended meaning.

Review Video: Reading Comprehension: Using Context Clues
Visit mometrix.com/academy and enter code: 613660

Substitution to Find Meaning

One way to find out if you have figured out the correct meaning of a new word is to **substitute** the meaning for the word. Using the example for *reluctant*, if the reader substituted in "not willing," the sentence would read

> Sam was "not willing" to be in the play, so he told the director that he was too busy to rehearse and didn't go to tryouts. He felt to shy to get up on a stage.

This is a way for the reader to confirm that they have used the context clues in the sentence correctly.

Synonyms and Antonyms

When you understand how words relate to each other, you will discover more in a passage. This is explained by understanding **synonyms**, which are words that mean the same thing, and **antonyms**, which are words that mean the opposite of one another. As an example, *dry* and *arid* are synonyms, and *dry* and *wet* are antonyms.

> **Review Video: What are Synonyms and Antonyms?**
> Visit mometrix.com/academy and enter code: 105612

Example

Read the following sentence from the *Secret Garden* by Frances Hodgson Burnett and determine the meaning of the word *pattering* based on context clues.

> "I like you! I like you!" she cried out, *pattering* down the walk; and she chirped and tried to whistle, which last she did not know how to do in the least.

In the example sentence, the words 'down the walk' show that the character is moving on a sidewalk. The reader knows that the character is crying out and trying to chirp and whistle while moving, so the character cannot be completely out of breath. The character is also trying to reach the person or thing that she is crying out to. from these context clues, the reader can guess that the word *pattering* means to walk quickly.

Example

Using context clues, determine the meaning of the word *pestilent* in the following excerpt from *Rip Van Winkle* by Washington Irving

> In fact, he declared it was of no use to work on his farm; it was the most *pestilent* little piece of ground in the whole country; everything about it went wrong, and would go wrong in spite of him.

In the example, the word *pestilent* is used to describe the ground. The character states that it was of no use to work on his farm and that everything about it went wrong. This indicates that the ground was difficult to work with, since the character had trouble with the ground no matter what he tried ('and would go wrong in spite of him'). The reader can assume, from these observations, that the word *pestilent* means troublesome, annoying, or not allowing anything to grow, since this example is about the ground on a farm.

Example

Read the following sentences and determine the meaning of the word *reluctant* based on context clues:

> Sam was *reluctant* to be in the play, so he told the director that he was too busy to rehearse and didn't go to tryouts. He felt too shy to get up on a stage.

In this example sentence, the words "too busy" show that Sam made an excuse about why he couldn't be in the school play. The sentence also says that he "didn't go to tryouts." the second example sentence has other clues. It says, "He felt too shy to get up on stage." These clues give the reader hints about what the word *reluctant* means. It means "not willing."

Definition Within a Text

An author may **define** a word in the text. For example, an author may write, "The company did not have sufficient capital, that is, available money, to continue operating." The author defined "capital" as "available money." Authors will use words and phrases, such as "that is," "or," "meaning," and "which is," to let the reader know that they are defining the word.

Analogy

Analogies are used to **compare relationships**. For example, the analogy "restaurant is to eating as store is to shopping." A restaurant is a place where you eat, and a store is a place where you shop. The analogy compares locations and the things people do at those locations. **Analogies** can also be used to show the meaning of unfamiliar words. For example, consider the analogy "author is to writing as artisan is to crafting." *Artisan* may be an unfamiliar word to some. However, this analogy begins with "author is to writing." An author writes to create books, articles, and poems. The first part of the analogy pairs a person's job title with the action that their job requires. Based on this, a reader can conclude that an artisan is someone who crafts things.

Examples that Clarify Meaning

An author may use a word and then give examples that reveal its meaning. Consider this text: "Those who do not know sign language can communicate with people who are deaf or hard of hearing by using gestures. These may include pointing their fingers to indicate which direction to look or go or holding up a hand to indicate stopping." The author of this text has used the word *gestures* and then followed it with examples. This shows a reader who is unfamiliar with the word that gestures are hand motions. Readers can find examples by looking for signal words like "for example," "for instance," "like," and "such as."

Multiple-Meaning Words

A multiple-meaning word has different definitions, depending on the contextual use of the word. A multiple-meaning word is also called a **homonym**. A homonym is defined as a word that has more than one meaning, but is spelled and pronounced the same for all of them. For example, look at the word *leaves* in the following two sentences:

1. Michelle *leaves* the building at 5 o'clock every day.
2. The *leaves* fell off the oak tree in September.

In the first sentence, *leaves* means exits. in the second sentence, *leaves* refers to parts of a tree. By looking at the rest of each sentence, the reader can understand which definition of the multiple-meaning word the author is referring to.

Similar Words

Homophones are words that are pronounced the same, but may be spelled differently. an example of two homophones would be *heir* (someone due to inherit an estate) and *air* (the invisible substance people breathe).

Homographs are words that are spelled the same, but may be pronounced differently. an example of a homograph is the word *row*, which is pronounced one way when used to mean a horizontal grouping and is pronounced another way when used to mean an argument.

Root Words and Affixes

A **root word** is a word that can be added onto. an **affix** is a prefix or suffix that is added onto a root word. Often, the affixes in the English language come from Latin or Greek origins. A **prefix** is added to the beginning of a root word and a **suffix** is added to the end of a root word. When you look at the meaning of a root word and the meaning of any affixes added to the root word, you can figure out the approximate meaning of the word. For example, the root word "happy" means "to be content." the prefix "un-" means "not." the reader can therefore figure out that "unhappy" means to "not being content."

Common Greek and Latin Root Words

Root	Meaning	Example
auto	self	automobile (a self-propelled vehicle)
geo	earth or ground	geography (study of the earth)
photo	light	photon (a small particle of light)
mis/mit	to send	transmit (to send something to another place)
bene	good	benefactor (a person who uses their resources for another person's good)
man	hand	manual (to do with one's own hands)
vac	empty, void	vacant (the state of being empty)
scrib/script	to write	transcript (a written copy of spoken words)
jur/jus	law	jurisdiction (the area in which a person can make judgements or rules)

Common Prefixes

Prefix	Meaning	Example
dis-	not	disagree (not agree)
im-	not	impossible (not possible)
in-	in, into, not	injustice (an action that is not just)
mis-	wrongly	misspell (to spell wrongly)
non-	not	nonpaid (not paid)

Prefix	Meaning	Example
pre-	before	preview (to view before)
sub-	under	submerge (to sink below the surface)
super-	over or greater than	superhuman (greater than a regular human)
trans-	across, through, or change	translate (to write or say in a different language)

Common Suffixes

Suffix	Meaning	Example
-able	can be done	likeable (can be liked)
-er	a person connected with	teacher (a person connected with teaching)
-ful	full of	wonderful (full of wonder)
-it/ity	state of	activity (state of being active)
-ive	cause to, tend to, or doing	creative (a person who tends to make new things or think of new ideas)
-logy	study of	biology (study of life)
-ment	the result	payment (the result of being paid)
-ness	state of being	darkness (being dark)
-y	characterized by	cloudy (characterized by clouds)

Example

Determine the meaning of the word "misconception" based on its root and affixes.

The word "misconception" is made up of three sections: a root, a prefix, and a suffix. to figure out the meaning of the word, you need to analyze these parts of the word individually. The root *concept* means "idea." It comes from the Latin word *conceptus* meaning "something conceived. There are two affixes in the word. The prefix *mis-* means "not" or "bad." the suffix *-tion* means "action" or "process." Put these meanings together and the word "misconception" means "the act of having a bad idea" or "misunderstanding."

Studying roots and affixes is important because it allows you to decode words that you might not otherwise understand with relative ease.

Chapter Quiz

1. A thesaurus can do all of the following, EXCEPT:

a. Give synonyms of words
b. Give word definitions
c. Help find the meaning of an unfamiliar word
d. Help authors vary their word choice when writing

2. Which of the following are words that sound alike, but are spelled differently and have different meanings?

a. Synonyms
b. Antonyms
c. Homophones
d. Homographs

3. What common suffix indicates state of being?

a. -ness
b. -y
c. -ful
d. -er

Chapter Quiz Answer Key

1. B: See section **Thesaurus**

2. C: See section **Similar Words**

3. A: See section **Common Suffixes**

Comprehension Skills

Making Predictions

When you read a story, you should look for clues to make a prediction about what will happen. At the end of the story, you may even think about what will happen next to the main character, and use the clues in the story to make a prediction. You can also use personal experience to help make a prediction.

Suppose there is a story about a boy going swimming, and he swims too far out. Suppose the story says the boy can't get back to shore and starts to yell. Suppose the lifeguard comes and helps him. Suppose the story stops after the boy goes back in the water again. The reader might make the prediction that the boy won't swim as far out this time. This may not be true, but it is the most likely thing to happen.

Example

Describe what prediction can be made based on the following sentences:

> When Glen is sick, his mother keeps him home from school. He stays in bed all day and takes medicine. Glen woke up this morning with a sore throat. His head was hot, and he felt achy.

The story says that Glen's mother keeps him home when he is sick and that Glen spends the day in bed when he is sick. The story says that Glen woke up this morning with a sore throat. His head was hot, and he felt achy. The reader can figure out that Glen was sick. Because Glen's mother always keeps him home when he is sick, the reader can predict that Glen will be staying home from school and spending the day in bed.

You can also use text features find information to make predictions and verify conclusions determined about different texts. Using key words as clues, looking for bold print words, looking for sentences that include captions, and words that are written in italics are a few features that can be used to help understand and make predictions about a text.

Using Structure and Genre to Make Predictions

The structure and genre of a story can also help readers make predictions. Most stories follow the same structure. They have an exposition, rising action, a climax, falling action, and a resolution. Because most stories follow this structure, readers can predict that each of these parts will occur in the story. For example, rising action usually begins after the conflict of the story is introduced. This means that if characters have not faced any conflict, the reader can predict that something will go wrong for the characters. Likewise, stories in the same genre may contain similar events. For example, in a mystery, the characters work to solve a crime or explain a strange event. So, when reading a mystery, the reader can predict that the conflict will be a crime or event that the characters must learn more about.

Making Connections to Enhance Comprehension

Reading involves thinking. For good comprehension, readers make text-to-self, text-to-text, and text-to-world connections. Making connections helps readers understand text better and predict what might occur next based on what they already know, such as how characters in the story feel or what happened in another text. Readers can make connections before, during, and after reading. Venn diagrams and other graphic organizers can help readers visualize connections.

Text-to-Self

Reading while looking for connections with the reader's life and experiences makes literature more personally relevant and meaningful to readers. Sentences showing text-to-self connections may begin with these examples:

- This reminds me of a time when...
- I understand how the character feels because...
- The setting makes me think of...
- I experienced this same thing when...

Text-to-Text

Reading while looking for connections to other texts helps the reader learn to identify the way authors use genre, setting, characters, plot elements, literary structure and devices, and themes to create meaning. Sentences showing text-to-text connections may begin with these examples:

- The character in this story reminds me of the character in...
- These two stories are alike because...
- The conflict in this story is similar to the conflict in...
- The relationship between the friends in this story is different than the relationship in...

Text-to-World

Reading while looking for connections to the world helps the reader begin to see literature as a reflection of real life and notice patterns in history and current events. Sentences showing text-to-world connections may begin with these examples:

- The event in this story sounds like the event in history when...
- The actions of this character sound like...
- This is like what happened in real life when...
- I heard about this on the news when...

Making Inferences

An **inference** is a **conclusion** or generalization that the reader makes based on the information provided within a text. Certain facts are included to help a reader come to a specific conclusion. It is what the story may hint about, and what a reader can conclude as a result of what the author says in the passage. It is also the best guess that a reader can make based on what happened or was said or in a story. A good inference is based on or supported by details in the passage.

Readers may come to their own conclusion about a topic, or the author may state a conclusion at the end of a story. When readers are in the middle of a story, they can predict what will happen at the end of it based on the events that have occurred so far and the typical characteristics that have been presented by the author up to that point. A reader needs to consider all of the information that an author has presented, including the main point and supporting points, to make logical conclusions and inferences about the story.

For instance, if a passage says that Joan is holding her mouth and moaning, you might conclude, or **infer,** that she has a sore mouth or a toothache. You cannot be sure of this, but it is the best conclusion that you can reach using the information at hand. Inferences are considered **implicit information**. They are not found directly in a passage, but they can be supported by explicit information from the passage.

Review Video: Inference
Visit mometrix.com/academy and enter code: 379203

Finding Explicit Information

Explicit information is the term for information that is **directly stated** in a story or passage. It is what **the author tells you**. It is not information that is hinted at or that you have to make a conclusion about. Explicit information can be facts or details about an event, something or someone. There is usually a lot of explicit information in a story and this information is often used to make an inference or draw a conclusion. to answer questions that ask about explicit information, simply reread the story until you find the answer. in fiction, details about characters, events, and setting are often explicit.

Example

Read the following excerpt and tell what information is explicit.

> From his bed, Steve could see the moon begin to rise and the stars twinkle. He could hear the nurses as they walked down the long hall, their footsteps echoing in the quiet.

The explicit information in the excerpt is all about Steve and what he could see and hear. The passage says that he could see the moon begin to rise and the stars twinkle from his bed. It also says that he could hear the nurses walking down the hall. This is explicit information. The author is describing what Steve can see and hear. There is nothing that is hinted at in the excerpt except that Steve seems to be in a hospital. However, that conclusion is not explicit information. The author does not say this directly, so it is implicit information.

Example

Read the following excerpt and tell what you can conclude about why Vicki got a cold.

> Hi Nance,
>
> Richard and I went camping last weekend. A bear ate all our food while we were sleeping. and it was cold and rainy the last night. We have both caught colds. Next time we go camping we are going to bring warmer clothes and extra food for the bears.
>
> Love, Vicki

You can conclude that Vicki got a cold because it was cold and rainy on the last night of her camping trip. She also talks about bringing warmer clothes the next time she goes camping, which further suggests that she was cold. However, the fact that a bear ate her food would have little to do with her getting sick, so that is not the reason she got a cold. It is logical to conclude that she got a cold because of the weather and not having warmer clothes. It is the best inference that you can make from the letter. Inferences are the best guesses that a reader can make based on the information in a passage.

Example

Read the following sentence. Draw a conclusion based upon the information presented:

> The hilltop was covered in low-lying clouds of grey, and a moist silence hung in the air as if the sky had drawn in a breath and paused.

The reader can conclude, or infer, based on the information in the sentence, that it is about to rain on the hilltop. The words used in the sentence give the reader clues to draw this conclusion. For example, the words low-lying clouds of grey indicate that rainclouds are present. A moist silence often occurs just before a storm. Based on the reader's own experience and the words presented in the sentence, the reader can conclude that the storm is about to break. Authors will often only present a certain amount of detail to the reader, and the reader needs to fill in the blanks. an author will give the reader just enough information to come to a logical conclusion without having to directly state that conclusion in the story.

Implicit Information

Implicit information is information that is **not directly stated** in a text, but can be inferred from something that the author explicitly states. For instance, the author may say "Seth buys a new TV, laptop, and home theater system every year." from this the reader could infer several things. For instance, Seth probably likes electronics and has a lot of spending money.

Example

Draw a conclusion based on the implicit information in the following sentence from the *Adventures of Tom Sawyer* by Mark Twain:

> He had discovered a great law of human action, without knowing it—namely, that in order to make a man or a boy covet a thing, it is only necessary to make the thing difficult to attain.

The reader can clearly see from the sentence that the character did not set out to learn something, but through an action, the character learned that people will want what is hard to attain. Although it's not explicitly stated, the reader can draw the conclusion that the character gained the experience of coveting (or desiring) something that was hard to get.

Key Ideas and Supporting Details

Identifying **key ideas** helps the reader see what a text or story is mostly about. They are the **most important ideas** in a text, and everything else in the text builds around and supports them. Every piece of writing has key ideas. The **supporting details** in a story, such as the characters, events, and settings, will work together to reveal the key ideas. The details are not key ideas, themselves. They make the key ideas clear and show the reader the author's purpose for writing the text.

Synthesizing a Text With Existing Knowledge

Synthesizing is similar to summarizing but it takes it one step further. Synthesizing involves taking the main points of a text and comparing it with existing knowledge to create a new idea, perspective, or way of thinking.

Another term for knowledge that you already have is **schema**. The plural form of this word is **schemata**. Schemata contain all the ideas you have about something. Synthesizing is all about how schemata change over time with the introduction of new information.

Example

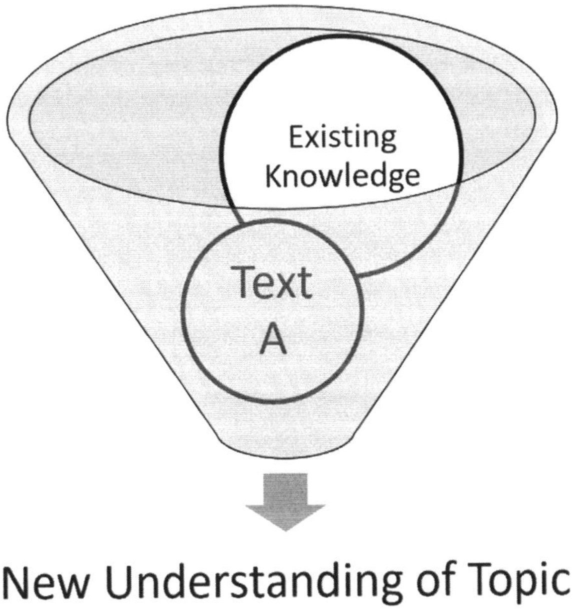

Using self-questioning strategies can help readers synthesize texts with their schemata to increase or change their understanding of topics. These questions include

- What do I already know about this topic?
- Is any of this new information?
- Has my perspective changed now that I've read this?
- What do I understand now that I didn't before?
- What are the main ideas of this text?
- How do the parts of the text fit together to create meaning?
- Are there any text-to-text, text-to-self, or text-to-world connections here?

Synthesizing Texts Without Existing Knowledge

If the reader is completely unfamiliar with the topic, they will have no background knowledge. in this case, instead of using existing knowledge, synthesizing may instead be done by combining the ideas provided in two or three different texts. The reader must make connections between the texts, determine how the ideas fit together, and gather evidence to support the new perspective.

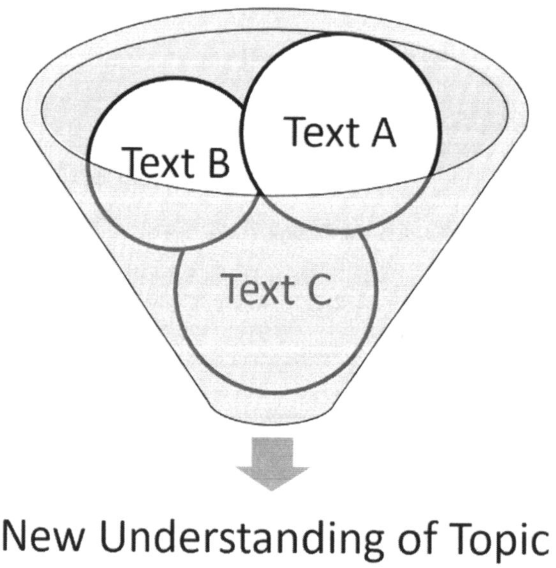

Using self-questioning strategies can help readers synthesize texts to increase their understanding of topics. in this case, readers are creating new schemata as they read. Common questions include:

- What do these texts have in common?
- What is different between these texts?
- What new information have I learned?
- What do I understand now that I didn't before?
- How do these texts relate to one another?
- If I think of these texts as parts of one whole, what meaning do they create together?
- What predictions can I make about this topic?

Chapter Quiz

1. Which of the following helps the reader learn to identify ways authors use genre, setting, characters, plot elements, literary structure and devices, and themes to create meaning?

a. Reading while looking for connections to the reader's life
b. Reading while looking for connections to other texts
c. Reading while looking for connections to the world
d. Reading while looking for connections to history

2. Which of the following is a conclusion that the reader makes using clues in the text?

a. Thesis
b. Prediction
c. Inference
d. Guess

3. What term refers to knowledge that you already have?

a. Cognition
b. Glossary
c. Schema
d. Explicit information

Chapter Quiz Answer Key

1. B: See section **Making Connections to Enhance Comprehension**

2. C: See section **Making Inferences**

3. C: See section **Synthesizing a Text with Existing Knowledge**

Response Skills

Text Evidence

The term **text evidence** refers to information found in a text that supports a reader's claim about the text. A reader can draw conclusions or inferences based upon information found in a text. Often, the author will deliberately include information that supports the main point of the text to help the reader make conclusions and inferences that align with the author's purpose for writing the text.

Drawing Conclusions Based On Text Evidence

Readers often need to use prior experience and background information to draw an accurate conclusion about the passage they are reading. Sometimes interpreting the information in a sentence can be difficult, especially if the reader is unfamiliar with some of the words used in a sentence. Looking at the words that the reader does understand in the sentence can help. By taking a pen or pencil and underlining important information in a sentence, the reader can better understand what the author is trying to say and draw a clearer conclusion from that.

Example

Draw a conclusion based on the following sentence.

New Orleans then was a mere huddle of buildings around Jackson Square; but with the purchase of the Louisiana territory from France, and the great influx of American enterprise that characterized the first quarter of the last century, development was working like yeast...

The sentence describes how New Orleans grew after the "purchase of the Louisiana territory" and how "development was working like yeast". Yeast multiplies rapidly, so the reader can conclude that New Orleans was growing rapidly.

Example

Read the following sentence. Draw a conclusion based upon the information presented.

> "A rosy-faced servant-maid opened the door, and smiled as she took the letter which he silently offered."

The reader can conclude, based on the sentence, that the servant-maid is friendly. The words "rosy-faced" and "smiled" lead the reader to this conclusion. People who are friendly are often described as having rosy complexions and smiling as a common sign of pleasantness. The reader can also assume, from the sentence, that the letter does not present any threat or unpleasantness to the servant-maid. The person presenting the letter does not have anything to say upon offering it, so perhaps he is waiting to see how the servant-maid will react.

When interpreting a sentence, always look for key words that describe a character. The author carefully crafts a description of each character, to form a picture in the reader's mind about what the character is like.

Paraphrasing and Summarizing

Paraphrasing and summarizing are two ways readers can work to understand what they read. Both involve reading a text and recalling the main points in an accurate way, but they differ in several ways.

How to Paraphrase	How to Summarize
State the message in the text in the reader's own words, while keeping the original meaning of the text Take all of the original ideas and word them in a way that the reader can better understand Put what the reader has read into their own words, rephrasing what the author has written	State main points of the text clearly and to-the-point. Take information and state it simply, in a much shorter form. Put information in a short form that keeps the main points of the whole text. Do not include many details, just the main idea of the text

Paraphrasing is often done for individual ideas, while summarizing is done for an entire block of text or ideas. Often times, a summary can be done in just one sentence, boiling down the author's words into just main idea.

Review Video: Summarizing Text
Visit mometrix.com/academy and enter code: 172903

Paraphrasing the Main Point of a Sentence

Paraphrase the main point of the following two sentences:

> Emmanuel went swimming in the lake by his house, where the water reached a depth of twenty feet in the middle. He did not venture out more than six feet into the water, however.

When paraphrasing a couple sentences or an entire paragraph, always include the main point of the text being reviewed, this is what the reader needs to know about the text. in the example, the reader needs to know that Emmanuel went swimming in the lake, but not more than six feet out. A paraphrase of the text may include: Emmanuel went swimming six feet out in the lake by his house. That is the main point that the audience needs to know.

Recall that a paraphrase is stating the author's ideas in the reader's own words. A summary typically involves including the main points of a longer text, such as a novel or full story.

Example

Read the following paragraph and then give a one sentence summary statement:

> When choosing a pet, people need to think about what type of home they can offer the animal. For example, a small apartment might not be a good fit for a large dog, but could be

a comfortable home for a kitten. A house that has a big yard would be great for a puppy, but a rabbit does not need a large yard.

In order to summarize, one has to identify the main idea and any supporting ideas in the author's work. The summary is an overview of the author's paragraph and will tell what it is about without getting into any of the details. The summary needs to be broad enough to cover all of the information in the author's paragraph. Here is a possible summary statement for the above paragraph:

> People need to consider a number of factors, particularly the available space they have, when choosing a pet.

Example

Read the following sentences and then paraphrase the material:

> Phillipe is debating which elective he should take next year. He is considering choir, band, and soccer. He is making a list of pros and cons to talk about it with his mom so that he is sure to make the right choice.

When paraphrasing information, one needs to read carefully and pay attention to details, then put the material away and write or tell it in their own words. One does not want to look at the material while paraphrasing to avoid plagiarizing by accident. Here is one example of a way to paraphrase the sentences:

> Phillipe has to choose a new elective for his schedule. His choices are choir, band, and soccer. He wants to make the right choice, so he's making a list of pros and cons and planning to talk to his mom.

Summarizing Literature to Support Comprehension

When reading literature, especially demanding works, summarizing helps readers identify important information and organize it in their minds. They can also identify themes, problems, and solutions, and can sequence the story. Readers can summarize before, during, and after they read. They should use their own words, as they do when describing a personal event or giving directions. Previewing a text's organization before reading by examining the book cover, table of contents, and illustrations also aids summarizing. So does making notes of key words and ideas in a graphic organizer while reading. Graphic organizers are another useful method; readers skim the text to determine main ideas and then narrow the list with the aid of the organizer. Unimportant details should be omitted in summaries. Summaries can include description, problem-solution, comparison-contrast, sequence, main ideas, and cause-and-effect.

Chapter Quiz

1. If a reader takes an author's original idea and then restates it, putting the idea into their own words, this is an example of:

a. Outlining text
b. Paraphrasing text
c. Summarizing text
d. Abstracting text

2. Which of the following is NOT true of summarizing?

a. A summary can be just one sentence that boils down the author's words into the main idea.
b. Summarizing helps readers work to understand what they have read.
c. A summary typically involves restating the main points of a text in a simpler, shorter fashion.
d. A summary should be subjective and include brief personal opinions on the subject.

Chapter Quiz Answer Key

1. B: See section **Paraphrasing and Summarizing**

2. D: See section **Paraphrasing and Summarizing**

Literary Elements

Theme

The **theme** of a story is the lesson that it teaches, or the message the author wants to get across. The theme is linked to the characters, the setting, and the events in a story. A passage can have two or more themes that convey its overall idea.

The theme of a story is not the same as the topic of a story. The topic is what the story is about, but the theme is what a reader is meant to learn. When readers are discussing theme, they can determine both theme topics as well as theme statements.

Theme topics are broad ideas that apply to the text. Examples are:

- Love
- The importance of friendship
- Good vs. evil
- The circle of life

Themes may also be complete statements written in sentence form. Examples are:

- Acts of courage can bring positive changes to the world.
- True friendship can withstand the hardest challenges.

Some themes are fairly common. These themes are called **universal themes** and they suggest things about life, society, and human nature.

Themes are very rarely stated in the text. Instead, the reader has to **infer** the theme by reading closely and thinking carefully about what the author is saying.

Themes are an important part of literature because they serve the purpose of teaching the reader or listener a truth about life. The theme is developed by how a character or characters respond to their situations and challenges.

Example

Explain why "Take care of what you care about" accurately describes the theme of the following excerpt.

> Luca collected baseball cards. But Luca wasn't very careful with them. He left them around the house. His dog liked to chew. Luca and his friend Bart were looking at his

> collection. Then, they went outside. When Luca got home, he saw his dog chewing on his cards. They were ruined.

This excerpt tells the story of a boy who is careless with his baseball cards and leaves them lying around. His dog ends up chewing them and ruining them. The lesson is that if you care about something, you need to take care of it. This is the point of the story. The theme is the lesson that a story teaches. Some stories have more than one theme, but this is not really true of this excerpt. The reader needs to figure out the theme based on what happens in the story. Sometimes, as in the case of fables, the theme is stated directly in the text. However, this is not usually the case.

Example

Read the following passage and explain why "It is better not to run away" describes the story's theme.

> Ivan made fun of Sasha. So Sasha was scared of him. If he saw Ivan coming, Sasha hid. Then Sasha changed. He stopped hiding from Ivan. If Ivan laughed at him, Sasha laughed right back. He wasn't afraid anymore. Soon, Ivan stopped making fun of Sasha. This made Sasha feel happier.

The theme "It is better not to run away" fits what happens in the story. Sasha is scared of Ivan and hides from him. But then Sasha stops hiding and laughs back at Ivan, and after that he is not afraid anymore. For him it was better not to run away, but to stay and face his fears. in the end Sasha is happier. He solved his problem. This is the theme that the story teaches through the events of the story. Sasha and the reader learn that something good happened when Sasha did not hide or run away. This is the message of this passage. The reader needs to figure out the theme from what happens in a story.

Characters

Character Trait

The traits of a character may include how they act and physical characteristics; a character trait is a behavior or physical characteristic that is unique to a specific character. For example, a character may be outgoing, which means he or she likes to talk a lot, or they may have bright red hair. These are both character traits.

An author uses character traits to describe a character in a story and help the reader to learn more about how the character acts and what they look like. By comparing the character traits in a story, the reader can see similarities and differences between characters. The author includes character traits to help the reader understand why a character may act a certain way in the story. For example, a character who is shy may not want to talk with a lot of people in a new classroom, but a character who is outgoing may want to talk with many people.

An author typically provides many details about a character so that the reader can learn more about the character's traits, motivations, relationships, and any conflicts they may have in the story. The traits of a character may include how they act and how they look. Characters are often motivated by things that have already happened in their life or how they feel about a topic. The author will often give the reader enough information about the character so that the reader can figure out why the character responds to a situation in a certain way. The author will also often give details about the relationships between characters and points they may conflict on. For example, a character may be good friends with another character; however, the two characters may disagree on where to play outside if one character likes being near the water and the other character does not.

Example

Read the following description of a character and decide, logically, whether the character is likely to go hiking outdoors:

> Jeremy lived in a high-rise in Chicago. He was studious, and not very athletic. Jeremy preferred to stay indoors and read a book, rather than enjoy outdoor weather.

Based on the description of the character's traits, preferences, and personality, he is not likely to go hiking outdoors. The description indicates that the character prefers reading, rather than enjoying outdoor weather. In addition, the character lives in a tall building in the middle of a large city, in order for him to enjoy the outdoors, he would have to travel away from where he lives. The character is not likely to change his preferences. A situation may lead the character to go hiking, but he is not likely to initiate the action on his own. A description of a character that is likely to go hiking outdoors may include a preference for outdoor activity and living near trails.

Character Relationships

A relationship is the way one character acts with another character in a story. The characters are often called **major characters** if they have a main part in the story and **minor characters** if they have a smaller part. There are many different kinds of relationships. For example, two children in a story may be friends, but they could be angry with each other, competing with each other, or helping each other. An author may tell the reader what kind of relationship the characters have. An author might give hints about a relationship. For example, the author may show one child making fun of the other child, which would suggest that the two children do not have a friendly relationship. The author might show one child teaching the other child how to read, which would suggest that the two children have a friendly relationship.

Example

Read the following sentences and describe the relationship Jill and Anna have:

> Jill came over to Anna and asked if she wanted an apple. "Sure, I'd love one. Thanks," Anna answered. Anna took a bite of the apple and started to chew it. Her chewing was so loud that they both started to laugh.

The author does not tell what the relationship between Jill and Anna is. The reader must figure it out from their actions. These actions are the clues the author gives. Jill asks Anna if she wants an apple. Anna says yes and starts to eat it. Her chewing is very loud. Both Jill and Anna start to laugh. They seem to like each other. Jill seems generous to Anna because she gives Anna an apple. They laugh together, and friends often laugh together. The reader can use personal experience to decide that it seems as though Jill and Anna are friends.

Character Changes and Responses

Characters can change in a multitude of ways throughout a story; however, there are main aspects of a character that change. A character's identifying **characteristics**, such as personality or behavior traits, may change as the result of a prominent event in the story, current **motivations**, and conflicts. As **conflicts** change or are resolved, a character may no longer be motivated by striving toward a goal that was previously important to them. Furthermore, a character's development may also lead them to make **different choices**, which can **impact the plot**. As the plot of a story moves along, characters can constantly change in relation to events that occur. Relationships between characters and the points of view of characters may change throughout a story as well.

Each story will have many different types of characters and each of these characters will have a different relationship with other characters. Stories usually have a protagonist, antagonist, and a variety of other characters including round, flat, and stock characters.

Protagonist

The main character in a drama, movie, novel, or other fictional text. The author portrays the protagonist in a way that the audience is most like to identify with themselves. The protagonist is generally undertaking some type of personal challenge throughout the story. The author writes the story so that the reader becomes aware of the protagonist's emotions and is generally able to empathize with the personal challenge.

Antagonist

The character that actively opposes the protagonist by trying to prevent them from succeeding. The antagonist is usually presented in such a way as to make the audience dislike them, and want them to fail at stopping the protagonist. The protagonist and antagonist oppose each other, so their relationship is almost always one of dislike.

Flat Characters

Does not have any substantial changes throughout the story. They stay the same despite the conflict, and do not learn any lessons. They are usually minor characters that might interact with the main character in some way.

Round Characters

Major characters in the story that will be more fully developed than other minor characters. They will usually encounter some type of conflict that they must overcome, and usually learn a lesson about life or themselves along the way.

Stock Characters

Often get their characteristics and mannerisms from stereotypes of people that are widely recognized. These types of characters are often repeated and well-known. Readers should be aware that stereotypes are rarely accurate in reality, and are generally intended to be humorous or dramatic. Some examples are evil stepmothers, unintelligent blondes, rude athletes, and loyal servants.

PLOT

The storyline of any text is also called a **plot**. The characters and events in the story determine what the plot will be. Readers may find a **plot line** useful as they try to put the events in the text in order and determine the relationships between events.

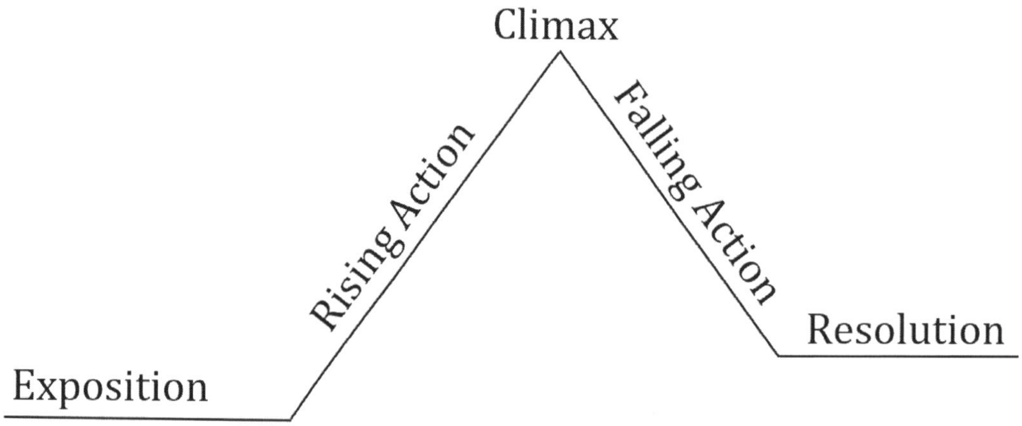

Review Video: Plot Line
Visit mometrix.com/academy and enter code: 944011

Every plot will begin with **exposition**, which introduces the characters and the setting of the story. The plot will continue to develop as new ideas and events centered on the main conflict in the story are revealed, which is called the **rising action**. The action in the story will rise until a **climax** is reached within the conflict. The climax can also be referred to as the turning point in the story, since the climax is where each character makes an important decision. After the climax, the action starts to wind down during the **falling action**. At this point, the characters begin to follow the paths they chose in during climax. The events of the story reach **resolution** in some way by the end of the story. Some conflicts are left open-ended, so that the reader is left to decide what really happened at the end of the story. Keep in mind that not all resolutions are happy or peaceful.

EXAMPLE

Read the following plot and analyze what event is missing from the plot sequence.

> Martin's family decided to go camping at the local park over the weekend. They packed all the camping necessities and drove to the park. Thick sheets of rain poured down all day, so they were stuck in their tent.

Martin and his family forgot to check the weather forecast before they left for their camping trip. to fill in the missing detail, the author may write: "Martin and his family checked the forecast and saw that it was going to rain, but decided to go camping anyway." the flow of the story is broken up by the sudden realization that it is raining, something that could be prevented by adding in the missing detail.

When details are missing from a plot sequence, the audience has trouble following the action in a story. By adding in additional details, the point of each step in a story can be made clearer to the audience.

CONFLICT

An important part of analyzing the plot of a passage is identifying the **main conflict**. There will likely be many smaller conflicts in the story, but there will be one main problem that influences the characters and events. to identify the main conflict, first look at who the main character is. Now ask yourself what they want. They may want to something to happen or not happen, another character to do or not do something, or to confront or avoid a problem, among other things. Once you know what they want, now ask yourself what is standing in the character's way. It may be a person, an event, or something less tangible like the passing of time. Combining what the main character wants and why they do not currently have leaves the reader with a summary of the main conflict.

Review Video: Conflict
Visit mometrix.com/academy and enter code: 559550

EXAMPLE

Read the following sentence from the *Call of the Wild* by Jack London and describe the main conflict in the sentence. Explain how the conflict may be resolved.

> The breaking down of discipline likewise affected the dogs in their relations with one another.

Based on the information in the sentence, an event has caused the dogs, the characters in the story, to not follow their regular routine. The sentence indicates that there has been a breaking down of discipline which is affecting how the dogs relate to each other. in order to solve this conflict, discipline needs to be restored. However, in order to return to previous relations between the dogs, any problems that are in the way of conflict resolution need to be taken care of. The word *likewise* means *also*, which tells the reader that other parts of the story are being affected besides the relations between the dogs.

EXAMPLE

Read the following sentence and explain the main conflict between the two characters:

> Joe stared angrily at Jamie's retreating back as Jamie raced away down the field with Joe's soccer ball.

The main conflict in the sentence is that Jamie has Joe's soccer ball. There may be additional conflicts between the two characters, but none are evident from the evidence shown in the sentence. in any story, a conflict may be minor and only affect part of the story, or be the main focus, taking an entire story to solve a conflict between characters. in the context of the sentence, it is not clear whether or not the entire story will revolve around Jamie taking Joe's soccer ball.

RESOLUTION

The term **resolution** usually indicates the result of a conflict in a story. Conflict between characters, within a character, or against an external element is necessary in order to have a plot for a story. without conflict, no events would occur to form the story. A conflict will come to a climax, and then conclude in some way. The resolution of a problem may be open-ended, end tragically, or end in a way that is good for everyone involved. The problem resolution typically occurs near the end of a story, after the climax has happened. A problem may be resolved by the characters involved within the conflict or by an external event; an upcoming resolution may be foreshadowed in the text, or may be completely unexpected by the reader. If the resolution is completely unexpected, it is considered to be a **twist** in the story.

NON-LINEAR PLOT DEVELOPMENT

Some texts contain a **non-linear plot**, which means the plot is not told in chronological order, or is not told from "beginning to end" in one straight line. There are several devices that authors can use to make their plot non-linear, including:

- **Foreshadowing:** the author gives the reader hints early on in a work about something that will become clearer (or more important) later on.
- **Flashback:** the author shows the reader an event that happened in the past to explain something about the present.
- **Subplot:** a side story, usually about a supporting character, is told along with the main story. Sometimes subplots occur within flashbacks.
- **Parallel plot:** two stories are told alongside each other, often narrated by two different characters in alternating chapters. The events in the stories usually end up overlapping or coming together at some point, most often the climax of the text.

SETTING

The setting is the **time** and **place** in which a story **takes place**. The setting of a story may stay the same for the entire story or change as events in the story unfold. For example, an entire story may take place in one room or cross continents as the reader follows the characters along on a trail of events.

The setting of a story is described by the author in terms of what it looks like, how the character feels, and anything else that is happening at that location at the time. For example, a character may be caught on a doorstep on a cold, rainy day. The character may feel frustrated as they shiver in the doorway, waiting for the heavy rain to let up a bit.

SHAPING A CHARACTER WITH SETTING OR PLOT

The setting of a story shapes character because it helps to define the situation that a character finds herself in. A character is limited to the setting of a story. For example, if a story takes place in a cold environment filled with snow and ice, this is certain to impact what actions a character can and will take. Frequently, the setting changes the way characters behave based on time. For example, the character of a woman who is a single mother in 1920 would be seen and behave very differently than a single mother in 2020.

EXAMPLE

Read the excerpt and determine how the setting influences the character in this excerpt.

> She had swum too far out. The waves were higher than she thought. She was struggling hard to get to shore. She wondered if she would make it. She thought of her childhood. Had she been right to run away from home, she wondered? Just then, a lifeguard grabbed her and helped her to shore.

The setting of the ocean and the high waves creates a conflict in the character. She is worried. She thinks about her childhood and her parents. She doesn't know if she will make it to shore. This is how the setting affects the character in this excerpt. without the high waves and the struggle, she would not become so worried and start to think about her past. She probably would not have questioned herself. This is an example of how a setting influences a character. If the waves had not been high, there probably would not have been a struggle or any self-searching of the swimmer's past.

HISTORICAL AND CULTURAL SETTING

Historical context influences literature in a number of ways. The style of the author's writing can be impacted by the historical period during which it was written (e.g., Dickens wrote at a time when authors were paid by the word; this is why his novels are so long). Obviously, the setting of the book includes its historical context. in addition, dialect may be a function of the historical period of the book. When a reader understands the historical context of a particular book, he or she can have a deeper understanding of the novel. Knowing about the time period during which the author wrote, as well as the time period discussed in the novel, helps the reader understand some of the author's choices, including character motivations.

PATTERNS RELATED TO SETTINGS

The setting of a story can allow the reader to draw on personal experience about where the story takes place. If a story takes place on a farm, the reader will likely picture a rural, peaceful setting, which may go along with (or be in contrast to) the actual plot of the story. For example, a reader would not expect a scary story to occur on a farm on a sunny day. Conversely, a reader may view a dark subway as a dangerous place, while the plot of a story set there may be based on a very calm series of events. When an author is crafting a story, they need to consider what the audience may already think about a particular setting in order to properly present the events of a story for greatest impact.

CHAPTER QUIZ

1. What type of character often gets their characteristics and mannerisms from stereotypes of people that are widely recognized?

a. Minor characters
b. Stock characters
c. Flat characters
d. Round characters

2. Every plot will begin with ____________, which introduces the characters and the setting of the story.

a. Conflict
b. Rising action
c. Foreshadowing
d. Exposition

3. What plot device that authors can use to make their plot non-linear, is a side story told along with the main story?

a. Anecdote
b. Flashback
c. Subplot
d. Parallel plot

4. Which of the following would most likely convey a peaceful setting to the reader?

a. Sunny farm
b. Damp basement
c. Loud construction site
d. Dark subway

CHAPTER QUIZ ANSWER KEY

1. B: See section **Stock Characters**

2. D: See section **Plot**

3. C: See section **Non-Linear Plot Development**

4. A: See section **Patterns Related to Settings**

Literary Genres

LITERARY GENRES

Literature contains many different **genres**, which are categories that texts can be divided into. Genres are used to group types of writing together for purposes of study, reading, or simple organization. Some common literary genres are

- **Realistic fiction** -A story that could actually happen and reflects life in a realistic way.
- **Adventure stories** -Short, mostly fictional stories that follow characters as they go on an adventure or quest.
- **Historical fiction** -Often strays from historical reality in order to tell a story and make a true historical event more interesting to the reader.
- **Mysteries** -Fiction stories about solving crimes or revealing secrets.
- **Humor** –Stories, mostly fictional, full of fun and excitement meant to entertain readers. Can be seen in stories from all genres.
- **Myth** -A legend or traditional narrative, often based on a historical event. The story reveals something about human behavior or the natural world, and often involves actions of gods.

POETRY

POET VERSUS SPEAKER

The author of a poem is called a **poet**. Many poems are written in first person, which means the **stanzas** (groups of lines) include words like "I" and "me." However, the poet is not always the **speaker** of the poem. In a novel, the author can create characters with different points of view. The characters can argue or have different roles to play in telling the story. Similarly, a poet may write a poem from a different point of view or even include more than one voice. The speaker is the voice of the poem, and is not always the same person as the poet him or herself. The reader or listener should know that the person telling the story is a character, and not always a real person.

For example, this excerpt from a poem by Dr. Seuss reads:

> When you think things are bad,
> when you feel sour and blue,
> when you start to get mad...
> you should do what I do!
> Just tell yourself, Duckie,
> you're really quite lucky!
> Some people are much more...
> oh, ever so much more...
> oh, muchly much-much more
> unlucky than you!

Even though one line has the word "I" in it, the poem is not from the perspective of Dr. Seuss. He is the author of the poem, but not the speaker. The person saying "I" is a character, just like in a story.

Sensory Language in Poetry

Sensory language is when the author uses descriptive words and specific details that appeal to a reader's senses (sight, touch, taste, hearing, smell, emotion). For example, the author can use scents that the reader is familiar with to help them imagine what the setting of the poem smells and feels like. This use of sensory language is also called **imagery**.

Rhyme in Poetry

Poets use rhymes to help readers understand poems. Words **rhyme** when they sound similar to each other, especially when the similar sound is at the end of the words, like *cat* and *hat*, or *roar* and *soar*. Rhyming words usually have endings that are spelled the same way, but sometimes they are spelled differently, like *wait* and *hate* or *bear* and *snare*.

Famous poet Shel Silverstein uses rhyme in many of his poems. For example, in his poem "Listen to the Mustn'ts", the last word of the first- and second-lines rhyme with each other, and the last word of the third- and fourth-line rhyme with each other.

> Listen to Mustn'ts, child, listen to the Don'ts.
> Listen to the Shouldn'ts, the Impossibles, the Won'ts.
> Listen to the Never Haves, then listen close to me.
> Anything can happen, child, Anything can be.

The pattern of the rhymes in this poem forms a **rhyme scheme**. Sometimes poets use a rhyme scheme that makes every other line of the poem rhyme instead.

Line Breaks in Poetry

Line breaks are used to end a line of poetry. Poets use **line breaks** to control the **length** of **each line**. The length of lines in a poem can impact the poem's meaning and the **speed** at which the poem is read. **Long** lines are usually read more **quickly**, while **short** lines cause the reader to briefly pause and look to the next line, so their reading is **slowed**. These effects often contribute to the reader's experience when reading the poem, so poets aim to make the effects match the tone of their message in the poem.

Drama

Dramas are texts that are written to be performed by people reading the lines or acting the stories out. They can also be presented as monologues (one character speaks), dialogues (two character speak to each other), or pantomimes (body movements are used instead of spoken words). Dramatic texts are called plays or **scripts**, and they are written differently than other texts.

Text Structure in Drama

Plays are divided into **acts** (large units) and **scenes** (small sections inside acts) instead of chapters. There are also **stage directions**, which are instructions from the playwright about where items go, where actors should move, and what the characters should be doing during the scene. Stage directions are usually in italics to set them apart from other parts of the play. When it is time for a character in a play to speak, there will be **character tag** on the left side of the page which shows the name of the character (all letters of the name are capitalized) followed by a colon.

Here is an example of how a page from a play might look:

Title of Play

Act Number

Scene Number

The setting of the scene is being described here. The reader is being introduced to the characters and the things happening around them. Characters will enter speak to one another during the scene.

CHARACTER 1:

I am speaking. These are words I say. *(stage directions)* I am still speaking.

CHARACTER 2 *enters and does something.*

CHARACTER 2:

Now I am speaking. This is my dialogue.

Dialogue and Stage Directions

Dialogue refers to what the characters say in a play when they are talking to each other, talking to themselves, or even talking to the audience. The type of speech, word choice, and accent a character uses is specific to the role he is playing. For example, a person cast to play a cowboy would have certain words in his vocabulary that a character from a big city in the North would not have.

A playwright also uses stage directions to make the play flow smoothly. Character interaction helps the viewer to understand the mood of the scene. If two characters are confrontational, the viewer is aware that there is some type of conflict occurring. Stage directions create order when all the characters are on stage together.

Informational Text

Controlling Idea

The controlling idea, also called the main idea or thesis, of a passage is usually located in the first paragraph or two of text. Having the controlling idea near the beginning of the passage allows the author to grab the reader's attention and let them know what the rest of the passage will discuss.

To find the controlling idea in a passage, there are questions the reader can ask while reading: What is this passage about? What does the author want the reader to know about the topic? The supporting details will provide evidence that the controlling idea is correct and are found in the body of a passage. The supporting details often provide examples of the controlling idea.

For example, a passage may contain the controlling idea: "Ellis Island was an entry-point to America for many immigrants during the Industrial Revolution." A supporting detail for the controlling idea may be "Immigrants were examined for contagious diseases at Ellis Island before being granted entry to America."

Review Video: Thesis Statements
Visit mometrix.com/academy and enter code: 691033

EXAMPLE

Determine the controlling idea the following sentence tells the reader and indicate what details support the controlling idea:

> Her breath billowed out in clouds of white and disappeared into the quiet air.

The controlling idea is what the author wants the reader to understand about the text. Details help to explain or support that controlling idea. A controlling idea usually states the point of an entire essay, article, or book, but can be simply stated in one sentence. The controlling idea in the sentence above is that a girl is outside in the cold. Details to support this statement include the word 'her,' showing that the character is a girl, and 'clouds of white,' which indicate that the air is cold. in order to conclude that the girl is out in the cold, the reader needs to understand that breath can be seen when the air is cold.

SUPPORTING DETAILS

Authors use supporting details to provide evidence and backing for the main point. All texts contain details, but they are only classified as supporting details when they serve to reinforce some larger point. Supporting details are most commonly found in informative and persuasive texts. in some cases, they will be clearly indicated with words like **for example** or **for instance**, or they will begin with words like **first**, **second**, and **last**. However, these special words are not a requirement. As a reader, it is important to consider whether the author's supporting details really back up his or her main point. Supporting details can be factual and correct but still not relevant to the author's point. Sometimes, supporting details can seem important but they might not support the controlling idea in the story well because they are based on opinion that cannot be proven.

EXAMPLE

Decide whether the following sentence is the main point or a supporting point of a text, and state where the information would be placed in an outline:

> One type of horseback riding, bareback horseback riding, involves sitting on a moving horse without a saddle and grasping the horse's mane.

This sentence is a supporting point, with the main point of the entire text likely about horseback riding in general. As a supporting point, this sentence would go further down in an outline, next to any numeral after numeral I. This sentence can be followed by additional sub-points that further explain the concept of bareback horseback riding. When a supporting point is used to clarify a main point or topic, the supporting point helps to break the topic down into smaller pieces.

STRUCTURAL FEATURES OF INFORMATIONAL TEXT

Texts which intend to inform the reader about a topic are often accompanied by visual aids or graphics. Some common examples are listed below.

- **Forewords** appear before the actual text. Usually, forewords are not written by the author of the text. They are written by a different person who is well-respected in a related field of work or study. The author of the foreword usually provides some information about the texts and explains why they support the text.
- **Prefaces** are written to provide the reader with supporting information that was not included in the text. This information may help the reader better understand the text or may show the reader why the topic of the text is important or interesting to the author.

- **Introductions** usually appear as the first paragraph in a text. An introduction is used to catch the reader's attention and let the audience know what the text is about and how the topic will be covered by the text.
- **Insets and sidebars** show additional information related to the text in boxes or on the sides of the page. Insets can contain pictures or text, and sometimes have different colored backgrounds or font types to make them stand out from the text.
- **Visual aids** include features like diagrams, graphs, and charts. These can help the user think about information in a different way. They do this by visually presenting the relationship between the information in the text.
- **Bullet points** list items separately, making facts and ideas easier to see and understand.
- **Numbers** can also be used to list separate items. Usually, numbers are used to show that the items are part of a sequence. For example, in a list of instructions, each instruction may be numbered to show the reader the order in which each instruction should be completed.
- **References** are the sources of the information the author included in the text. In most works, the references will all be listed after the last page of the main text. These may be included on a page titled "Bibliography," "Works Cited," or, simply, "References." Reviewing the author's sources and reviewing their credibility can show the reader whether the work itself is credible, unbiased, and accurate.
- **Acknowledgements** appear near the end of books, after the main text and any resources that the author has included for the reader. The acknowledgements section is used by authors to thank the people that helped them create the work. People who encouraged the author, assisted the author with writing and editing, or made it possible for the work to be published are usually named in the acknowledgements section.

Organizational Patterns

When writing there are a variety of ways that an author can choose to organize their text. It is important for them to choose the pattern that best presents their information, as not all patterns will work for every piece of writing. Some examples are:

Advantage/Disadvantage

The author chooses a topic or concept and addresses both the advantages and disadvantages (or pros and cons) of the subject. in this type of text, the author is not trying to persuade their audience to choose a side, but rather, to inform the reader of all the possible positive and negative effects.

Cause and Effect

The author will write about relationship between two events that occur, where the second event occurs as a result of the first.

For example, a text may discuss a school policy stating that when a student is late to school too many times, they receive a detention. Later in the text, we might see a student repeatedly arriving late to school, after which he is given a detention. in this example, the **cause** is the student being late to school, and the **effect** is the student receiving a detention.

Classification

The author chooses a topic and divides it into smaller parts or groups in order to discuss them individually. These types of texts address how parts work within a whole, or what characteristics can be used to classify a given subject or concept.

Chronological Order

the author organizes the progression of events based upon when they occurred and what was included in each step of the story. By organizing the text in this way, the author presents all necessary information about the six questions readers can ask to help themselves understand the text: who, what, when, where, why, and how.

Compare and Contrast

The author will show similarities and differences between items or events.

For example, the author may write about cats and dogs. They might start by giving a brief description of the two. Then they will want to point out all of the similarities, such as; they both have tails, and both are kept as pets. Next, they will explain the differences, such as; dogs are canines, while cats are felines. They will try to provide as much detail as possible about both the similarities and the differences.

Definition

Authors introduce a concept or word and then explain or describe it. This type of text often included examples that will help the reader gain understanding of what is presumably a new concept for them.

Order of Importance

The author puts the information in the text in order of what is most important. Order of importance can be either increasing or decreasing, depending on how the writer wants to structure the work.

Problem and Solution

The author presents some information as a problem and then discusses a solution or attempted solution to that problem. In problem and solution, there is generally one main problem, but that one problem may have several possible solutions.

For example, suppose Billy wants a new video game but does not have the money. There are several possible solutions to this. He might try asking his mom to buy it for him. If that does not work, he could offer to do small jobs to earn enough money to buy it. A third possibility might be to wait until his birthday and ask for it then.

Identifying Organizational Strategies

Example

Explain which organization pattern would be the best choice for this writer and why.

> Sara is writing a report on sea turtles. She has researched the various dangers that they face: their predators, the difficulties they encounter in their life cycle starting with their birth, their migration to the ocean, and the dangers that await them as they mature. She is unsure of how to organize her report.

A cause and effect order would seem to be the best idea for Sara because she would be able to identify the causes and effects of the dangers that sea turtles encounter. She could organize the report so that each paragraph deals with a different threat, using headings to identify what would be in each section. A chart would also be useful because it puts the same information in a clear format so that readers would be able to refer to it. She might also consider using a video showing baby turtles migrating towards the open sea, which would give her audience an even greater understanding of the turtles' plight.

EXAMPLE

Identify the text structure that is used in the following sentences:

> Madison and her brother Jake used to live on a wind-torn island in the Chesapeake Bay. Last year they moved to Baltimore, a city in Maryland. Next summer they plan to visit the island where they grew up.

Chronological order is used as a text structure in the example sentences, as they are organized according to the passage of time. Note that each sentence refers to a point in time. The first sentence refers to where the siblings lived in the past. The second sentence refers to the siblings' move to Baltimore last year. The final sentence refers to what the siblings plan to do in the future. By referring to a specific place in time, the reader can see what occurred in the story during that time period. an author will often use flashback to indicate what happened in the past, and foreshadowing to give the reader a glimpse of what may occur in the future.

EXAMPLE

Identify the text structure that is used in the following sentences:

> Three cousins lived in the same small town. One day the cousins decided to journey together to enter a singing contest across the country. The cousins won the contest and made their hometown fans proud.

The information in the story can be organized according to the passage of time, called chronological order. The story will start based in the cousins' hometown, to give some background on where the cousins come from. Subsequent events in the story will occur over time based on the cousins' motivations due to their background. The story will end by referring back to how far the cousins have come from their small-town roots.

ARGUMENTATIVE TEXTS

IDENTIFYING THE CLAIM

In a persuasive or argumentative text, the author is writing in order to make and support a claim. A claim is similar to the key idea of an informational text. However, a claim can be argued, which means that some readers may not agree with it. The author of the text will need to use the body of the text to support the claim and show readers why they should agree with it. To identify the claim of a text, first identify the topic. Then, read the introduction text to see what the author writes about the topic.

The claim should be clearly stated in the introduction. However, if the claim is still not clear, read the body to see what kind of evidence the author uses to support the claim. The way that the author gives and applies evidence may also show what the claim of the text is.

CALL TO ACTION

Another strategy is to look for a call to action in the text. A call to action is a statement that instructs the reader to do something after reading the text. Often, the call to action will tell the reader to do something that shows that he or she agrees with the author's claim. For example, if an author's claim is that reading is better than watching a movie, the author may include a call to action that says "Turn off the TV and dig in to a new book today!" By including this statement, the author is telling the readers to show their agreement by choosing to read rather than watch a movie.

Identifying How the Author Supports a Claim

In a persuasive or argumentative text, the author must use information to support his or her claim. This information is called evidence. Below are common types of evidence an author may use to support a claim:

- **Facts:** Authors may use facts that show that their claim is true. For example, a claim that fish are better pets than dogs can be supported by the fact that fish cannot make a mess inside a house.
- **Personal Anecdotes:** A personal anecdote is a story from a person's own experience. Authors can use personal anecdotes to tell stories that show why their claim is true. For example, an author can support the claim that people should wear elbow pads when riding a bike can be supported by sharing a story about their experience of scraping their elbow after falling off of a bicycle.
- **Statistics:** Statistics are observations that are based on a collection of data. Statistics can show trends or preferences among members of a group. An author can use statistics to support a claim by sharing the statistic says is likely to happen or be true for many people.
- **Examples:** Authors may give examples of events or experiences that suggest that their claim is true. For example, an author may claim that people should exercise because it will make them healthier. The author could give an example of how exercise can improve a person's health in order to support this claim.
- **Quotes:** An author can support a claim by using quotes from other people or texts. If the person or text makes a statement that shows that the author's claim is true, the author can include that quote in his or her text. When authors include quotes in their work, they must always tell the reader where the quote came from.

The author must use enough evidence to support the claim. If the evidence does not fully support the claim in the text, then the author must continue working to find evidence for the claim. The evidence used to support a claim must also be believable and come from a reliable source.

Identifying the Intended Audience

Authors of persuasive and argumentative texts want to convince others to agree with a claim or take a certain action. Because of this, they will often write to a specific audience. Often, the target audience will include people who disagree with the author's claim. The author's desire is to give these people information that will lead them to change their minds or actions.

Strategies for Identifying the Intended Audience

One way to identify the intended audience of a persuasive or argumentative text is to first identify the author's claim. Then, consider who would disagree with the author's claim. This group of people is likely the group that the author wants to persuade.

Another way to identify the audience is to look for clues in the text. Sometimes, authors will clearly state which people are included in the intended audience. For example, imagine that an author includes the statement, "Teachers should reward their students every time they make a good grade on a test." This shows that the text is written to persuade teachers who do not already reward their students for good test grades. Similarly, a call to action may show who the target audience is by instructing the members of the audience to take a certain action.

Chapter Quiz

1. Literature in what genre is often based on historical events, reveals something about human behavior or the natural world, and often involves actions of gods?

a. Historical fiction
b. Myth
c. Fantasy
d. Adventure

2. In dramatic texts (plays or scripts), which of the following are usually in italics to set them apart from other parts of the play?

a. Dialogues
b. Acts and scenes
c. Stage directions
d. Character tags

3. What structural feature is used to list items separately, making facts and ideas easier to see and understand?

a. Boldface
b. Bullet points
c. Sidebars
d. Headings

4. In what organizational pattern does the author choose a topic and then divide it into smaller parts or groups in order to discuss them individually?

a. Deductive
b. Inductive
c. Classification
d. Definition

5. If an author writes about cats and dogs, showing their similarities and differences, this would be an example of what type of organizational pattern?

a. Cause and effect
b. Problem and solution
c. Proposition and support
d. Compare and contrast

6. In an informational text, when is the main idea of a passage often presented?

a. In the first sentence
b. In the first one to two paragraphs
c. In the middle
d. At the end/conclusion

Chapter Quiz Answer Key

1. B: See section **Literary Genres**

2. C: See section **Text Structure in Drama**

3. B: See section **Structural Features of Informational Text**

4. C: See section **Classification**

5. D: See section **Compare and Contrast**

6. B: See section **Controlling Idea**

Author's Purpose and Craft

Author's Purpose

The author's purpose his or her reason for writing the text. As the readers read a text, they should always try to figure out the author's purpose for writing as this will help them to better understand the message that the author is trying to convey.

Informational Texts

- Inform the reader on a topic that they previously knew nothing about, such as many non-fiction texts.
- For example, an informative paper on early Native American Indian tribes would detail where Native American Indians lived, what types of foods they ate, how they bartered for goods, and other aspects of their culture.

Persuasive Texts

- Influence the reader to think a certain way about a topic, calling them to action or pointing them toward resources that would help them to learn more about the topic.
- A **proposition and support** paper would be an example of this, where an author gives their opinion and then tries to convince the reader to see something from their point of view.
- For example, an author may try to persuade the reader that waterparks are the best place to go in the summer when it is hot outside. The author would present information about waterparks and explain why they are good places to visit.

Expressive Texts

- Express the author or speaker's opinion or emotions about a topic. Generally, expressive texts include descriptive words to clearly show the reader how the author or speaker feels.
- For example, the author of a poem may think that compassion is an important quality in a person, and they may write a poem in which the speaker discusses how compassion is what binds all people together.

Entertaining Texts

- Entertain the reader, such as in most fictional texts.
- For example, Wilson Rawls, the author of *Where the Red Fern Grows* entertains his readers with the adventures of a young boy named Billy and his two hound dogs, Old Dan and Little Ann.
- Entertaining texts can be either fiction or non-fiction, but are usually stories such as a fairy tale or fictional piece of writing. Entertaining texts usually follow a chronological order.

Authors usually write to entertain, to inform, or to persuade their readers. The organization structure or pattern they use is related to what the author's purpose is. It is important to choose the pattern that best presents the information, as not all patterns will work for every piece of writing.

Review Video: Understanding the Author's Intent
Visit mometrix.com/academy and enter code: 511819

EXAMPLE

Read the following sentence. State the author's point in writing the sentence, whether it is to inform, persuade, express an opinion, or entertain:

> The rollercoaster reached a peak and paused for a second, before gliding down the other side of the hill with a roar.

The purpose of the sentence is to entertain the reader. The author does not state his or her opinion on the topic, and the sentence doesn't inform the reader about an important topic. The sentence does not persuade the reader to accept a certain point of view, and is instead meant to entertain the reader by giving them the feeling they might get from riding an exciting roller coaster.

Notice that the text describes an event, rather than an issue or conflict. The event is part of a larger tale, where a series of events occur to form an entire story. The reader may notice that the author uses descriptive words to present the setting, such as gliding and roar. The reader can better picture a story when the setting is clearly presented.

EXAMPLE

Read the following sentence and state the author's point in writing the sentence, whether it is to inform, entertain, persuade, or state an opinion:

> The new student handbook makes it against the rules to wear roller skates inside the school buildings.

The purpose of this sentence is to inform the reader. The sentence does not state an opinion on the topic, nor is it meant to entertain the reader. The sentence also does not persuade the reader to accept a certain point of view. The sentence gives information to the reader that they need to know in order to avoid breaking the rules.

EXAMPLE

Read the following sentence from the *City of Ember* by Jeanne DuPrau and state the author's purpose in writing the sentence: whether it is to inform, entertain, persuade, or state an opinion:

> Lina looked out at the lighted streets spreading away in every direction, the streets she knew so well. She loved her city, worn out and crumbling though it was

The purpose of the sentence is to entertain the reader. The sentence does not tell the reader important information about a specific topic, it is simply used as part of a greater fictional story meant for entertainment. The sentence does not persuade the reader to accept a certain point of view, nor does it state an opinion.

When an author wishes to persuade the reader to accept a certain point of view, evidence is used to back-up a claim. If the author wants to state an opinion, that opinion is included within the text. Sentences that are meant to inform contain facts that the reader needs to know and are not often found in fictional stories.

PRINT AND GRAPHIC FEATURES

An author may show information in a chart, a graph, in paragraph format, or as a list. Information may also be shown in a picture or a diagram. The way an author chooses to show information is often based on the purpose of the text and the audience that the text is meant to reach.

A reader may be asked to answer questions based on the graphic by itself, how the graphic relates to the text, or how the text would best be shown in a graphic form. Some common examples of graphics are cause and effect organizers, circle graphs, bar graphs, illustrations, and diagrams.

Cause and Effect Graphic Organizers

Cause-and-effect graphic organizers are often used to map the **elements of a story**. A reader might read a story about a string of events and then be asked to correctly fill in either the **cause** or **effect** of an event in the story.

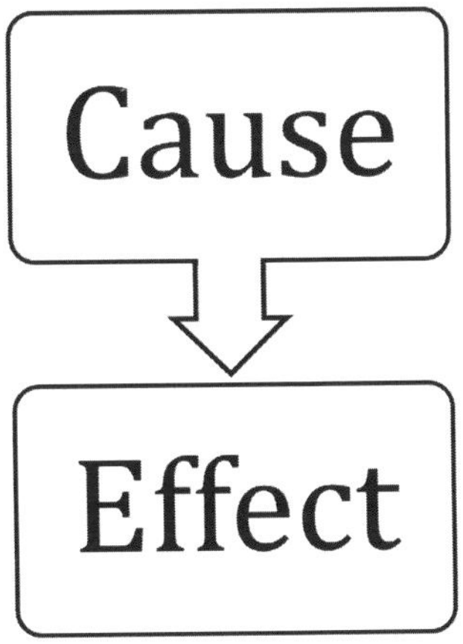

Example

Read the following excerpt from *Ramona Quimby, Age 8* by Beverly Cleary and decide what the cause of the hectic morning at the Quimby house is.

> With all four members of the family leaving at different times in different directions, mornings were flurried in the Quimby household.

A **cause and effect** graphic organizer for this excerpt might look something like this:

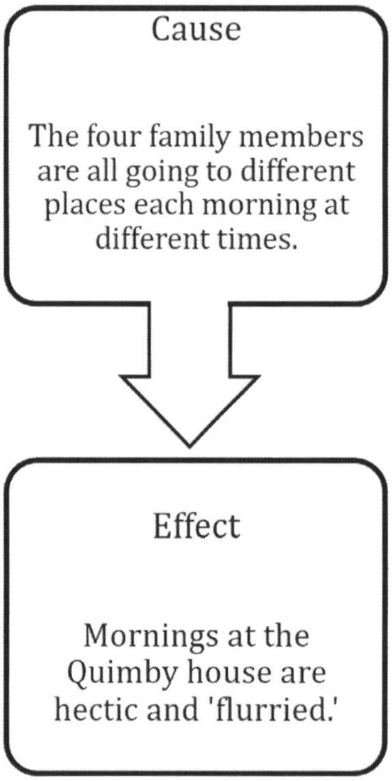

Line Graphs

Line graphs are used for measuring general **trends over time**. For example, this line graph shows an overall upward trend in the amount of candy bars sold for four weeks.

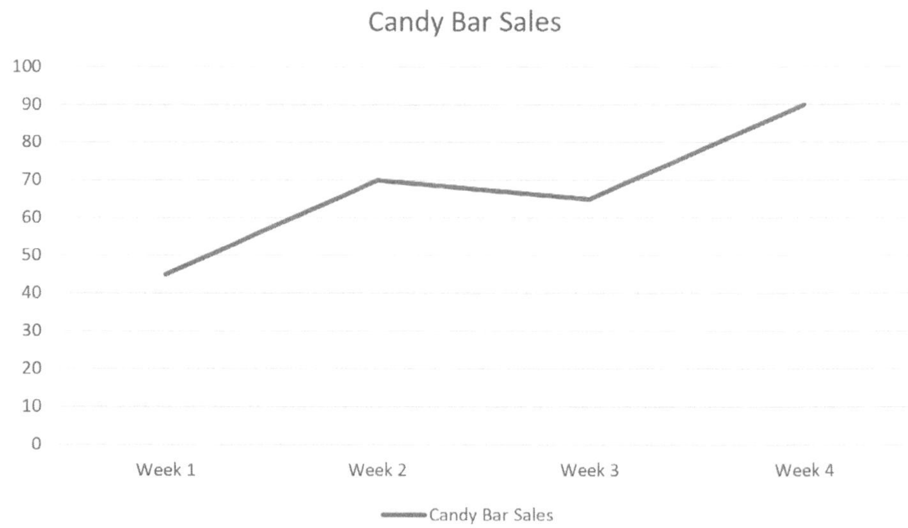

Circle Graphs

Circle graphs, also called pie charts, are often used to represent information that can be shown as **parts of a whole**. For example, this graph shows the results of people being asked about their favorite color:

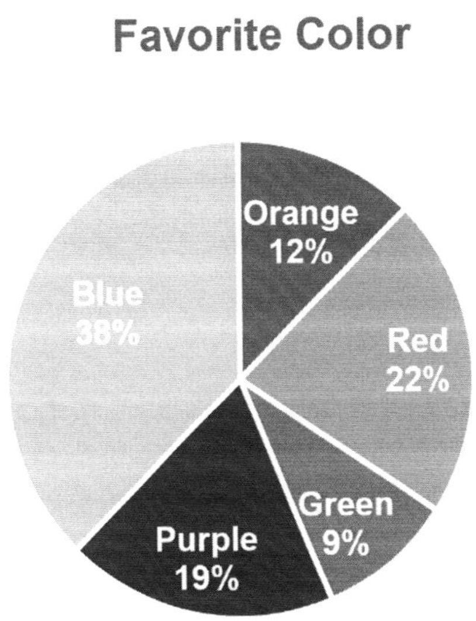

Bar Graphs

Bar graphs are used to show information about **numbers**. For example, this graph is a different way of representing the same results as those in the circle graph.

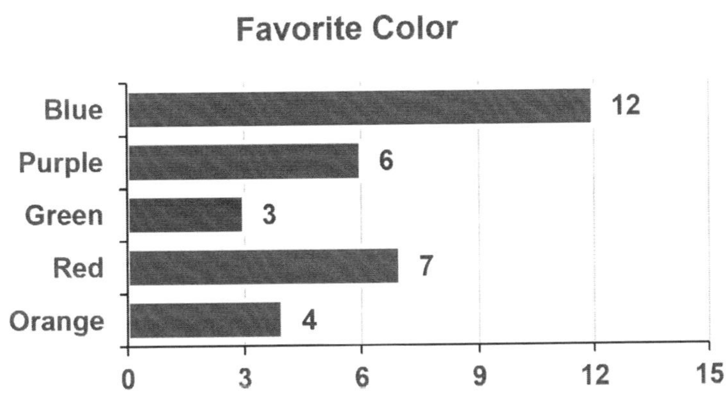

Illustrations and Photographs

Authors may choose to include **illustrations** or **photographs** (or both) with their texts. These two image types both show something from the text or give more information about the text.

Illustrations are drawings of an object. They may be based on reality, or they may represent an artist's abstract idea. For example, this is an illustration of a 1903 automobile:

Photographs are pictures of objects. They are generally extremely realistic, and most often show an object as it actually existed at that moment in time. For example, this is a photograph of a 1917 automobile:

Both illustrations and photographs give the reader another way to relate to and understand the text. The reader may be asked how the image relates to the text, what type of caption the image should be given, or why the author chose to include the image with the text.

Diagrams

Diagrams are used to show information in a visual way. There are many different types of diagrams, including:

Diagrams that show the parts of an object, how they work together, or how they should be put together. This is an example of a diagram which shows how gears turn together

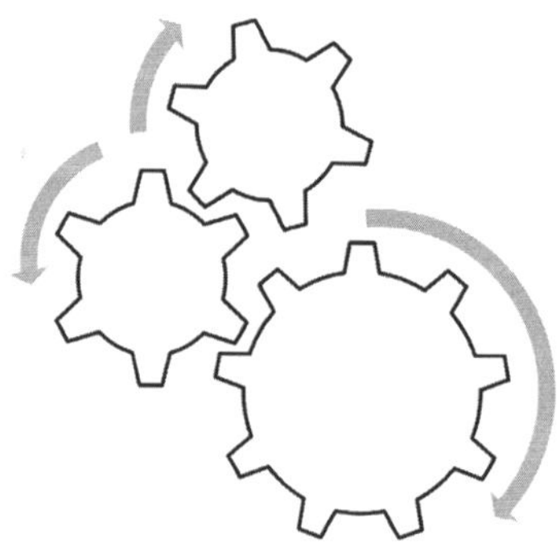

Diagrams that show how information is related are called **Venn Diagrams**. These are ways to visually see the way in which two different ideas overlap. This is an example of a Venn Diagram comparing cats and dogs:

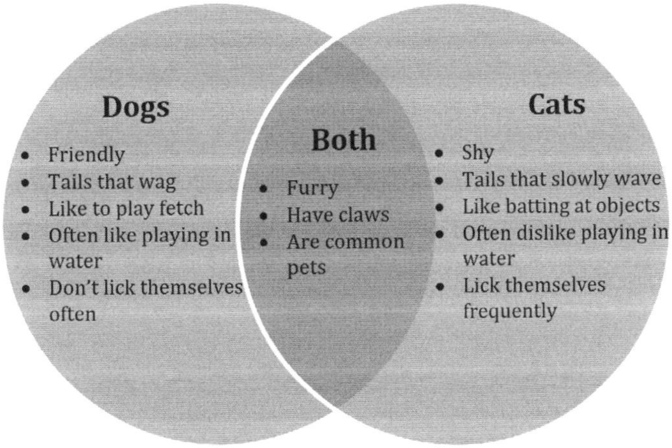

IMAGERY

Imagery is the use of **descriptive language** to add life or feeling to a work of literature. Many authors add literary and sound devices to create vivid pictures in the minds of their readers. Most of the time, imagery is thought to be one of the best ways to help readers fully understand and remember a work.

The most common forms of imagery are those that appeal to the sense of sight and sound. Imagery that appeals to the sense of sight, or **visual imagery**, helps the reader picture an event in their mind, usually by including specific details in the text that are not strictly necessary for the purpose of the story, but allow the reader to more easily "see" the scene. Some common forms of figurative language can help create visual imagery.

Review Video: Sensory Language
Visit mometrix.com/academy and enter code: 177314

LITERAL AND FIGURATIVE LANGUAGE

Many types of text use both **literal language**, which means just what it says, and **figurative language**, which allows the writer to expand the way in which he or she uses language. When an author uses figurative language, she connects things in an exaggerated and non-literal way in order to create a memorable image, which helps to describe a situation in a new way for the reader.

Review Video: Figurative Language
Visit mometrix.com/academy and enter code: 584902

SIMILE

- Shows similarity between two ideas or objects, using the words "**like**" or "**as**"
- For example, an author might write "The princess is as beautiful as a rose" to compare the appearance of a woman to a beautiful flower.

METAPHOR

- Puts one idea in place of another to draw a parallel between the two ideas.
- For example, an author might write "Her room was a pigsty," to compare a person's bedroom to a dirty spot where pigs sleep.

SYMBOLISM

- Using one object to stand for something else.
- For example, an author may include a flag flying high throughout a story to show pride in the characters' country and to represent the idea of patriotism.

HYPERBOLE

- An extreme exaggeration of an idea.
- For example, a character might say "I'm starving to death!" to show that they are really hungry. Most of the time a character who says this is not literally going to die from hunger, they are just ready for a snack.

IRONY

- Uses sarcasm or humor (usually with an emphasis on the opposite) to show difference from literal meaning.
- For example, if a character says "Well today must be my lucky day!" after they left their homework on the kitchen table, they are being ironic. The irony used here helps show that it is definitely *not* the character's lucky day.

PERSONIFICATION

- Gives life or human characteristics to an inanimate object
- For example, if an author writes "The trees whispered to each other across the wide blue sky," they are using personification to help the reader imagine the scene. Trees are not human beings, so they do not whisper, but the image created in the reader stands out more than a literal description would.

EXAMPLE

Based on current knowledge, identify whether metaphor, simile, or hyperbole is used in this sentence:

> The chiming bell was a beacon of hope for the downtrodden villagers.

A **metaphor** is used in this sentence to draw a parallel between "the chiming bell" and "a beacon of hope." the bell is being compared to something else in the sentence, which indicates the use of metaphor or simile, but the reader knows that the sentence does not contain a simile, because the words like and as are not used to show the comparison. The sentence also does not contain an exaggeration of facts, so the reader can see that hyperbole is not used.

EXAMPLE

Discuss the kind of figurative language used in the following poem by the Scottish poet Robert Burns:

> O my luve's like a red, red rose
> That's newly sprung in June;
> O my luve's like the melodie
> That's sweetly played in tune.

The poet uses **similes** to create an image in this poem. The two similes here occur when the speaker says that his love is "**like** a red, red rose" and that she is also "**like** the melodie." These are examples of similes because they use the comparing word 'like' to compare two things. They are not metaphors because metaphors do not use the comparing words 'like' or 'as.' the poem paints an image of the speaker's love by comparing her to a red rose that has newly sprung and a melody that is sweetly played.

EXAMPLE

Read the following excerpt from "The Raven" by Edgar Allan Poe, identify the metaphor, and discuss how it impacts the text:

> And the raven, never flitting, still is sitting, still is sitting
> On the pallid bust of Pallas just above my chamber door;
> And his eyes have all the seeming of a demon's that is dreaming

One **metaphor** in the excerpt from "The Raven" by Edgar Allan Poe is: "And his eyes have all the seeming of a demon's that is dreaming"

The metaphor compares the raven's eyes with a demon, which shows that the speaker thinks there is evil in the bird. The metaphor helps contribute to the overall tone of the poem and the reader's understanding of how the speaker views the bird.

EXAMPLE

Read the excerpt from a poem by William Blake and describe what form of figurative language it uses.

> The wild winds weep,
> And the night is a-cold;
> Come hither, sleep,
> And my griefs unfold.

This poem contains several examples of **personification**. in the poem, the speaker says "The wild winds weep," thereby giving the winds the human characteristic of weeping. Later it says "Come hither, sleep," which is another use of personification asking that sleep to go somewhere as though it were a person. The poem gives the winds and sleep human characteristics. This is the definition of personification. It is not an example of simile because there is no comparison using the words "as" or "like." It is not a metaphor because there is no comparison between two things sharing a similar quality. and it is not an example of hyperbole because there is no exaggeration. The poem does contain some alliteration, however; the repetition of the letter "w" in "wild winds weep" qualifies as alliteration, which is another literary technique.

POINT OF VIEW

The point of view of a text is the perspective from which it is told. Every literary text has a narrator or person who tells the story. The two main points of view that authors most often use are first person and third person.

FIRST PERSON

- Tells a story through the eyes of one character.
- Uses the pronouns 'I,' 'me,' 'we,' and 'my.'
- The reader gets only one side of the story, without any other angles on what may have happened in the text

Second Person

- Second person is an uncommon point of view in literature that uses the pronoun 'you.' Second person is usually reserved for speaking directly to someone, often when giving instructions.
- Examples might include: "Go get me a fork" or "will you wash the dishes?"

Third Person

- Tells a story about a character or group of characters from an outside viewpoint.
- Uses the words 'her', 'his,' 'they,' or a name to talk about a character or characters.
- A common way to show action in a story which allows the author to easily and realistically tell a story from more than one person's viewpoint.
- Gives readers a more complete view of a story as it is told from many different perspectives.

Different Forms of Third Person

When an author writes in third-person point of view, there are a couple of options to choose from:

- **Third person omniscient** - There is an all-knowing narrator telling the story as well as interpreting events, and relating thoughts of the characters.
- **Third person limited** - The author writes in the third person, but does so from only one character's point of view. There are two different variations of this type of narration: the narrator can either stay with the same character throughout or cycle through different characters over the course of the story.

Style, Voice, Tone, and Mood

Style, tone, and mood all play an important role in the development of a story. The reader's impression of a story can vary based on the style, tone, and mood established by the author.

- **Style** refers to the way an author uses words, phrases, and sentence structure. The style of the text can change depending on whether the author uses short, choppy sentences, long, elaborate sentences, formal language, or informal language.
- **Voice** refers to the characteristics of a text that show the author's personality and distinguish the author from other writers. An author's voice may be recognized through the way they use words or the way they organize and present their thoughts. Voice is specific to each writer, and it can be as specific and unique as personality.
- **Tone** refers to the attitude of the writer toward the subject matter. The tone can change throughout the text or stay the same. There are many ways to describe the tone of the text, such as light, playful, questioning, humorous, serious, solemn, or tense. The reader can identify the tone by paying attention to the author's word choice.
- **Mood** refers to the overall feeling conveyed by a setting. For example, a story may be dark in terms of setting, characters, and events that occur. If a story is presented in a picturesque countryside location where the characters are content and the style of speaking is elaborate, the reader will have a different impression of the story than if the setting is in a rundown house with a pale, unhappy caretaker that rarely speaks.

Review Video: Style, Tone, and Mood
Visit mometrix.com/academy and enter code: 416961

Rhetorical Devices vs Logical Fallacies

Writers of persuasive and argumentative texts will often use strategies that may help them persuade the reader to agree with their claims. These strategies may be used to convince the reader on a logical or emotional level. The writer may also use them to prove his or her own credibility, or reliability. These strategies are called **rhetorical devices**. However, writers make statements that seem like rhetorical devices, but are not actually logical. They may sound persuasive, but they are unreasonable and may leave out part of the truth or try to prove a weak argument. These are called **logical fallacies**.

Chapter Quiz

1. An author's purpose in writing fiction is most often to:

a. Persuade
b. Inform
c. Entertain
d. Express

2. What is the least common point of view, that tells a story using the pronouns "you"?

a. First person
b. Second person
c. Third person
d. Narrator

3. Which of the following refers to the overall feeling conveyed by a setting?

a. Style
b. Pace
c. Tone
d. Mood

4. What type of graphic can be used to visually see the way in which two different ideas overlap?

a. Circle graph
b. Bar graph
c. Venn diagram
d. Cause and effect organizer

5. What common form of figurative language puts one idea in place of another to draw a parallel between the two ideas?

a. Metaphor
b. Simile
c. Hyperbole
d. Irony

Chapter Quiz Answer Key

1. C: See section **Author's Purpose**

2. B: See section **Second Person**

3. D: See section **Style, Voice, Tone, and Mood**

4. C: See section **Diagrams**

5. A: See section **Metaphor**

Writing

Writing Process

Brainstorming

When choosing what to write about, activities like brainstorming can help inspire new ideas or help writers see how their ideas go together. **Brainstorming** means considering a variety of topics or ideas and is mainly used to find a creative approach to a subject or problem. A good first step in brainstorming is simple **free-association** with a topic. One way of doing this is sitting down with paper and pen and writing every thought that comes to mind about the topic in a word or phrase. It does not matter how helpful or good the thought seems at first; the writer should write down everything that comes to mind about the topic. Then, the writer should read the list over a few times. Next, he or she should look for patterns, repetitions, and clusters of ideas. This allows a variety of fresh ideas to come as the writer thinks about the topic.

Free Writing

Free writing is a more organized form of brainstorming. **Free writing** means taking a limited amount of time, like 2 to 3 minutes, to write everything that comes to mind about a topic in complete sentences. When the time is up, the writer should review everything he or she has written down. Many of the sentences may not make sense, but they may contain ideas and details that help the writer organize his or her ideas and prepare to plan the composition. Usually, free writing results in more useful ideas than brainstorming because the writer's thoughts and connections are written in complete sentences. However, both methods can be used together to help the writer prepare to plan and write a composition.

Mapping

One specific way to use graphic organizers is to map an essay. There are many different types of graphic organizers. One easy method to create one is to draw a circle in the middle of the page and write a broad topic in it. Then, draw smaller circles with related topics and ideas, or with topics that fit within the broad topic, written inside and draw line to connect each circle to the main circle. This method can show ideas that fit within the broad topic and will help guide the essay, or it can show which ideas may work better as the main topic of the essay.

Once the main idea and other ideas and details for the essay have been chosen, they can be used to map the essay. Mapping is another word for using a certain type of graphic organizer. These graphic organizers look like a map and organize ideas and details as they will appear in the essay. The essay map can have the main idea at the top or in the center. If the main idea is at the top, the supporting ideas will appear below it in a row, and any additional details will appear under the supporting idea they go with. If the main idea appears in the center, the supporting ideas may appear around it, and the additional details will appear around the supporting ideas they go with.

Planning

Planning is the process of organizing a piece of writing before writing a draft. At the beginning of planning, writers should decide **why they are writing** and **who will read what they write**. The writer must also choose a **genre**, which is the **type** of composition he or she will write. There are fiction genres, such as comedy, folklore, action, and mystery. There are also nonfiction genres, such as essays, reports, poems, and journals. To plan his or her composition, a writer may create an outline or a graphic organizer, such as a Venn diagram, a spider-map, or a flowchart. These methods should help the writer choose their topic, main ideas, and how to organize the composition. If the writer needs to do research for the composition, he or she may also do so as they plan. Planning helps writers organize all of their ideas and decide if they have enough information to begin their first draft. However, writers should remember that the decisions they make during planning may change later, so their plan does not have to be perfect.

DRAFTING

Writers may then use their plan, outline, or graphic organizer to compose their first draft. They may write more drafts after the first one to improve their writing. Writing multiple drafts can help writers think of different ways to state their ideas and correct mistakes that may be hard to fix without rewriting a section of the composition, or the whole composition. There is no "right" number of drafts, so different writers may write a different number of drafts. Writing drafts also makes it easier to write freely because a writer can improve his or her composition with each draft they write.

REVISING, EDITING, AND PROOFREADING

Once a writer completes a draft, he or she can move on to revising, editing, and proofreading to improve the draft. **Revising** is making sure that the composition is right for the audience, is not missing important information, is on topic, and is well organized. The writer should also consider the composition's style when revising and ensure that it is appropriately formal or serious. Revising may happen after the first draft so that errors are not repeated in the next draft. Each draft should be revised before the next one is written so that no mistakes are missed. **Editing** comes next. Editing a composition includes steps like improving transitions between paragraphs and making sure each paragraph is on topic. While editing, the writer must pay attention to the words he or she uses and the way the information in each paragraph is organized. Writers may also fix grammar mistakes in the editing phase, since some errors will require a writer to rewrite large parts of their work. **Proofreading** means fixing misspelled words, errors in grammar, and any other small mistakes in the composition.

During the revising, editing, and proofreading steps, it can be helpful for writers to ask a peer to read their work, since he or she may notice mistakes or problems the writer missed before. A writer may also choose to read his or her own work aloud, or listen to someone else read it. Hearing a composition aloud can help writers find mistakes or opportunities for improvement in their work more easily. This happens because when something is read aloud, the person reading the text must pay closer attention to the words on the page. When a writer or a peer reads the composition, they should point out any sentence that confuses them the first time they read it. Most of these sentences can be revised in a way that makes it easier to read and understand.

ADDING AND REMOVING INFORMATION

While both revising and editing may involve changing the words in a composition, they can also involve adding or taking away words. When a writer has completed a draft and reread it, he or she may notice that something, such as a transition, important details, or an explanatory sentence, is missing. Simply changing the words to make the passage sound better will not solve this problem, so the writer must **add** whatever words and information is needed to make the passage make sense and achieve the writer's purpose.

In other cases, a writer may have words, a sentence, or sometimes an entire paragraph that gives unnecessary information or explains the information in a way that is confusing. When this happens, the extra words and information weaken the composition and must be **removed**. Sometimes, this is difficult for writers to do because it may require them to remove writing they are proud of or a fact they find interesting. Despite this, revising and editing are steps meant to improve and strengthen a composition, so the writer should change, add, or remove parts of his or her writing in a way that makes it better and achieves his or her purpose.

Revising Sentences

Sentence variety is important to consider when writing an essay. A variety of sentence lengths and types can make an essay more engaging, and different types of sentences can sometimes help readers better understand information. For example, a sentence containing a list may make more sense when written with a simple sentence structure, since writing a compound sentence containing a list may give the reader too much information at once. On the other hand, information that is closely related and can be connected with a conjunction should be written in a compound sentence, rather than a simple sentence, since a compound sentence helps the reader see that the information goes together.

Using only simple sentences often makes writing boring and bothersome to read. Writing using only compound sentences makes it difficult for writers to explain information well and difficult for readers to understand, since every sentence will include a coordinating conjunction. To check an essay for sentence variety, it is helpful to look at whether the essay contains different sentence structures and lengths. It is also important to pay attention to the way each sentence starts and avoid beginning with the same words or phrases.

Revising Vocabulary

When writing informational or argumentative texts, it is important to use **precise vocabulary**, or **word choice**, to explain your main idea and supporting details. Generalized vocabulary will not help the audience fully understand the points that you are attempting to make because it will not accurately explain your main idea and supporting details. Precise vocabulary is important to use because it will accurately describe the ideas that are central to your text. When you research a subject, make sure to familiarize yourself with any vocabulary that is involved in its explanation. Use context clues, dictionaries, or, if necessary, a technical dictionary to decode any words that you are not familiar with. Precise vocabulary also impacts the effectiveness of narrative text. Carefully choosing vocabulary to describe sensory details, or imagery, helps writers paint the best possible picture of the events they are describing through their writing.

Chapter Quiz

1. Which of the following means taking a limited amount of time, like 2 to 3 minutes, to write everything that comes to mind about a topic in complete sentences?

a. Brainstorming
b. Drafting
c. Mapping
d. Free writing

2. What is often the first step after a writer completes a draft, and involves making sure that the composition is right for the audience, it is not missing important information, is on topic, and is well organized?

a. Adapting
b. Editing
c. Proofreading
d. Revising

3. When revising sentences in an essay, which of the following is NOT good advice?

a. Avoid beginning sentences with the same words or phrases
b. Include a variety of sentence lengths
c. Improve understanding by only using compound sentences
d. Keep sentences simple when they include lists

4. In what step of the writing process does the writer decide why they are writing, who will read what they write, and what genre they want to write?

a. Brainstorming
b. Drafting
c. Mapping
d. Planning

Chapter Quiz Answer Key

1. D: See section **Free Writing**

2. D: See section **Revising, Editing, and Proofreading**

3. C: See section **Revising Sentences**

4. D: See section **Planning**

Essay Structure and Organization

Controlling Ideas and Supporting Details

In the first paragraph of a composition, writers include a sentence that explains the **controlling idea.** This sentence is also known as the **thesis**. The rest of the paragraph shows the reader why the topic of the essay is interesting and includes details that support the controlling idea. One way to understand the relationship between the controlling idea and supporting information is to think about a table: the tabletop is the controlling idea, and each of the table's legs is a supporting detail or group of details. All of the legs work together to support the tabletop and create a table, just like the supporting details work together to support the controlling idea and create a composition.

Introduction

The introduction is used to capture the reader's attention and announce the essay's controlling idea. Normally, the introduction contains about 3-5 sentences. An introduction can begin with an interesting quote, a question, a strong opinion, or something else that will **interest** the reader's and prompt them to keep reading. If the composition has a prompt, the introduction should **restate** or **summarize** some part of the prompt so that the reader will have an idea of what information will be in the essay. Finally, your introduction should include the **controlling idea**, the primary thing the essay will tell the reader.

Review Video: Introduction
Visit mometrix.com/academy and enter code: 961328

Body

In an essay's introduction, the writer states the controlling idea and prepares the reader for the information in the rest of the composition. In the body of the composition, the writer **explains**, **demonstrates**, and **gives more information about** the **controlling idea**. This is done using supporting details and examples that are relevant to the controlling idea of the composition. For example, if the composition's controlling idea is a vacation the writer took, the body will include descriptions of where the writer went, what they experienced, and what they thought of the trip. If the composition's controlling idea is the writer's opinion, the body will include examples and facts that show why he or she has formed that opinion. If composition's controlling idea is a topic and the writer wants to instruct the reader, the body will contain facts, explanations, and examples that help teach the reader about the controlling idea. A writer will use supporting details to explain the controlling idea throughout the body.

The body should also contain multiple paragraphs, and the order the writer puts these paragraphs in is important. Each paragraph should include at least one supporting detail, but a paragraph may include more than one if two or more supporting details work together to support the controlling idea. If the controlling idea is to describe something that happened, the paragraphs should match the order in which the events occurred. If the controlling idea is to present an opinion or instruct the reader, the paragraphs should be ordered in the way that would make the most sense to the reader. The order of body paragraphs is important because it can impact how easy a composition is to read.

Review Video: Drafting Body Paragraphs
Visit mometrix.com/academy and enter code: 724590

Paragraphs

After the introduction of a passage, the body paragraphs will explain and elaborate upon the controlling idea. While each paragraph should relate to the controlling idea of the composition, each paragraph should focus on one point or supporting detail. Normally, a paragraph has a good topic sentence that summarizes the paragraph's main point. A topic sentence is a sentence that gives an introduction to the paragraph and its contents. Topic sentences should contain information that is more specific than what is in the introduction and may include a supporting detail, but they should not contain explanations or examples.

Supporting Details

The next sentences in the paragraph should support the topic sentence. These sentences can contain examples, explanations, or other specific information that supports the topic sentence, which supports the controlling idea of the composition. While a paragraph may be structured in any way, as long as it logically provides information that supports the controlling idea, it can be best to use a template or pattern to make sure that each paragraph is complete and well organized. For example, a good template to follow is topic sentence, evidence, explanation, conclusion. This means that after the topic sentence, the next sentence should provide evidence, like a quote or example, that supports the paragraph's main point. Next, the paragraph should include a sentence that explains how that evidence supports the paragraph's main point. If there are multiple examples or quotes, more than one sentence may be used to explain them. Finally, there should be a concluding sentence that helps the reader understand the paragraph and prepares them for the next one.

Choosing Supporting Details and Examples

When writing an informative or argumentative text, writers must choose supporting details carefully. Including details that are irrelevant, inaccurate, or vague does not strengthen the author's writing, while relevant, accurate, provable, and specific details do strengthen the author's writing. These details can make the writer's meaning clearer or give evidence that the author's points are true or logical. Such details may include examples or facts, such as statistics, statements from others who have authority on the subject, and common events or experiences. Choosing appropriate supporting details can also help the author show that they put effort into forming their ideas. This can also make the composition more intriguing and enjoyable to read, since the writer's own interest and insight will be apparent to the reader.

Length of a Paragraph

A paragraph must contain enough information to support its main point and the composition's controlling idea. A paragraph of two or three sentences will most likely not support the main point or controlling idea because it is not likely to contain enough information, explanation, or evidence. When a paragraph does not support the main point or controlling idea, it does not help the writer achieve their purpose or goal for writing the essay. A helpful, informative paragraph will often have somewhere from three to five sentences. Also, it is important that the sentences within the paragraph lead the reader through the information. Each paragraph should flow logically and stay on topic throughout.

Starting a New Paragraph

For most forms of writing, you will need to use multiple paragraphs. This means that deciding when to start a new paragraph is very important. Reasons for starting a new paragraph include:

- To separate the introduction and conclusion from the body paragraphs
- To move from one supporting detail or point to another
- To indicate an important shift in time or place
- To show a comparison, contrast, or cause and effect relationship

Coherent Paragraphs

A smooth flow of sentences and paragraphs without gaps, shifts, or bumps will lead to paragraph **coherence**. The connections between old and new information can be shown using several methods:

- **Clearly linking ideas**, from the topic sentence to the body of the paragraph, is essential for a smooth transition. The topic sentence states the main point, and this should be followed by specific details, examples, and illustrations that support the topic sentence.
- The **repetition of key words** adds coherence to a paragraph. To avoid dull language, synonyms of the key words may be used.
- **Parallel structures** are often used within sentences to highlight the similarity of ideas and connect sentences that give similar information.
- Maintaining a **consistent verb tense** throughout the paragraph helps make paragraphs coherent. Shifting tenses affects the smooth flow of words and can disrupt the coherence of the paragraph.

Review Video: How to Write a Good Paragraph
Visit mometrix.com/academy and enter code: 682127

Transitions

Transitions between sentences and paragraphs guide readers from idea to idea and show relationships between sentences and paragraphs. Writers should use transitions carefully and only when they are truly helpful. They should also be selected to fit the author's purpose. Transitions can show relationships such as time, comparison, an order of events, and cause and effect. Transitions are often used at the beginning of a phrase, sentence, or paragraph, since this helps prepare the reader for the next piece of information.

Review Video: Transitions in Writing
Visit mometrix.com/academy and enter code: 233246

Types of Transitional Words

Time	Afterward, immediately, earlier, meanwhile, recently, lately, now, since, soon, when, then, until, before, etc.
Sequence	too, first, second, further, moreover, also, again, and, next, still, besides, finally
Comparison	similarly, in the same way, likewise, also, again, once more
Contrasting	but, although, despite, however, instead, nevertheless, on the one hand... on the other hand, regardless, yet, in contrast.
Cause and Effect	because, consequently, thus, therefore, then, to this end, since, so, as a result, if... then, accordingly
Examples	for example, for instance, such as, to illustrate, indeed, in fact, specifically
Place	near, far, here, there, to the left/right, next to, above, below, beyond, opposite, beside
Repetition, Summary, or Conclusion	as mentioned earlier, as noted, in other words, in short, on the whole, to summarize, therefore, as a result, to conclude, in conclusion
Addition	and, also, furthermore, moreover

Review Video: Transition Words
Visit mometrix.com/academy and enter code: 707563

Conclusion

The conclusion of a composition should summarize the controlling idea and show that it has been explained well. A good conclusion shows the reader why the author's controlling idea is meaningful and important and how the supporting details should help the reader understand the controlling idea. The conclusion should also give the reader something to think about that is related to the controlling idea. For example, in the conclusion, the author can invite readers to think about how they feel or what they think after reading the composition. Some things to avoid when writing conclusions include:

- Introducing a completely new idea
- Apologizing for one's opinions or writing
- Repeating the controlling idea word for word rather than summarizing them
- Using the conclusion to summarize every detail in the composition

Review Video: Drafting Conclusions
Visit mometrix.com/academy and enter code: 209408

Chapter Quiz

1. "Too," "and," "next," "still," "besides," and "finally" are all what type of transitional word?

a. Time
b. Sequence
c. Comparison
d. Contrasting

2. Which of the following should be avoided in an essay conclusion?

a. Reminding the reader of the central idea by repeating it word for word
b. Showing the reader why the author's central idea is meaningful and important
c. Showing that the central idea has been explained well
d. Giving the reader something to think about that is related to the central idea

3. A helpful, informative paragraph will often have how many sentences?

a. One to three sentences
b. Three to five sentences
c. Five to ten sentences
d. Ten to fifteen sentences

4. The body of an essay should do all of the following, EXCEPT:

a. Introduce the central idea
b. Demonstrate the central idea
c. Explain the central idea
d. Give information about the central idea

Chapter Quiz Answer Key

1. B: See section **Types of Transitional Words**

2. A: See section **Conclusion**

3. B: See section **Length of a Paragraph**

4. A: See section **Body**

Grammar

Subjects and Predicates

Subjects

Every sentence needs a subject and a predicate. The **subject** of a sentence names who or what the sentence is about. The subject may be directly stated in a sentence, or the subject may be implied. The **complete subject** includes the simple subject and any **modifiers**, such as adjectives, articles, prepositions, and adverbs, that go with it. To find the complete subject, ask *Who* or *What* before the verb to complete the question. The answer, including any modifiers, is the complete subject. To find the **simple subject**, remove all of the modifiers in the complete subject.

Examples:

simple subject: car

The small, red car is the one that he wants for Christmas.

complete subject: The small, red car

simple subject: artist

The young artist is coming over for dinner.

complete subject: The young artist

Review Video: Subjects in English
Visit mometrix.com/academy and enter code: 444771

An imperative sentence is a sentence that gives someone instructions or makes a request to someone. In **imperative** sentences, the verb's subject is understood, but is not actually present in the sentence. For example, this about the sentence *Drive to the store*. This sentence is a command, and the subject is *you*. If the subject were directly stated, the sentence would be *You, drive to the store*. Another fact to consider is that, normally, the subject comes before the verb. However, the subject comes after the verb in sentences that begin with *There are* or *There was*.

Direct:

John knows the way to the park.	Who knows the way to the park?	John
The cookies need ten more minutes.	What needs ten minutes?	The cookies
By five o'clock, Bill will need to leave.	Who needs to leave?	Bill
There are five letters on the table for him.	What is on the table?	Five letters
There were coffee and doughnuts in the house.	What was in the house?	Coffee and doughnuts

Implied:

Go to the post office for me.	Who is going to the post office?	You
Come and sit with me, please?	Who needs to come and sit?	You

Predicates

In a sentence, there is always a predicate and a subject. The subject tells what the sentence is about, and the **predicate** explains or describes the subject.

Think about the sentence *He sings*. In this sentence, we have a subject, *He*, and a predicate, *sings*. This is all that is needed for a sentence to be complete. Most sentences contain more information, but if this is all the information that is given in a sentence, then it is a complete sentence.

Now, let's look at another sentence: *John and Jane sing on Tuesday nights at the dance hall.*

subject: John and Jane — predicate: sing on Tuesday nights at the dance hall.

John and Jane sing on Tuesday nights at the dance hall.

Subject-Verb Agreement

Verbs **agree** with their subjects in number. In other words, singular subjects need singular verbs. Plural subjects need plural verbs. **Singular** is for **one** person, place, or thing. **Plural** is for **more than one** person, place, or thing. Subjects and verbs must also share the same point of view, as in first, second, or third person.

Review Video: Subject-Verb Agreement
Visit mometrix.com/academy and enter code: 479190

Number Agreement Examples:

singular subject / singular verb

Single Subject and Verb: Dan (singular subject) calls (singular verb) home.

Dan is one person. So, the singular verb *calls* is needed.

plural subject / plural verb

Plural Subject and Verb: Dan and Bob (plural subject) call (plural verb) home.

More than one person needs the plural verb *call.*

Person Agreement Examples:

First Person: I *am* walking.

Second Person: You *are* walking.

Third Person: He *is* walking.

Complications with Subject-Verb Agreement

Words Between Subject and Verb

Words that come between the simple subject and the verb do not affect subject-verb agreement.

Examples:

The joy (singular subject) of my life returns (singular verb) home tonight.

The phrase *of my life* does not affect the verb *returns.*

The question (singular subject) that still remains unanswered is (singular verb) "Who are you?"

Don't let the phrase *"that still remains…"* confuse you. The subject *question* goes with the verb *is.*

Compound Subjects

A compound subject is formed when two or more nouns joined by *and, or,* or *nor* act together as the subject of the sentence.

Joined by And

When a compound subject is joined by *and*, it is treated as a plural subject and requires a plural verb.

Examples:

plural subject — plural verb

You and Jon are invited to come to my house.

plural subject — plural verb

The pencil and paper belong to me.

Joined by Or/Nor

For a compound subject joined by *or* or *nor*, the verb must agree in number with the part of the subject that is closest to the verb.

Examples:

subject — verb

Today or tomorrow is the day.

subject — verb

Stan or Phil wants to read the book.

subject — verb

Neither the pen nor the book is on the desk.

subject — verb

Either the blanket or pillows arrive this afternoon.

Indefinite Pronouns as Subject

An indefinite pronoun is a pronoun that does not refer to a specific noun. Different indefinite pronouns are used as a singular noun, a plural noun, or change depending on how they are used.

Always Singular

Pronouns such as *each*, *either*, *everybody*, *anybody*, *somebody*, and *nobody* are always singular. This is because these pronouns always stand in for one person, place, or thing.

Examples:

singular subject — singular verb

Each of the runners has a different bib number.

singular verb — singular subject

Is either of you ready for the game?

Note: The words *each* and *either* can also be used as adjectives. For example, *each* person is unique. When one of these adjectives modifies the subject of a sentence, it is always a singular subject.

singular subject — singular verb

Everybody grows a day older every day.

singular subject — singular verb

Anybody is welcome to bring a tent.

Always Plural

Pronouns such as *both*, *several*, and *many* are always plural. This is because these pronouns always stand in for more than one person, place, thing, or idea.

Examples:

> plural subject — plural verb
>
> Both of the siblings were too tired to argue.

> plural subject — plural verb
>
> Many have tried, but none have succeeded.

Depend on Context

Pronouns such as *some, any, all, none, more*, and *most* can be either singular or plural depending on what they are representing in the context of the sentence.

Examples:

> singular subject — singular verb
>
> All of my dog's food was still there in his bowl.

> plural subject — plural verb
>
> By the end of the night, all of my guests were already excited about coming to my next party.

Other Cases Involving Plural or Irregular Form

Some nouns are **singular in meaning but plural in form**: news, mathematics, physics, and economics.

> The *news is* coming on now.
>
> *Mathematics is* my favorite class.

Some nouns are plural in form and meaning, and have **no singular equivalent**: scissors and pants.

> Do these *pants come* with a shirt?
>
> The *scissors are* for my project.

Note: Look to your **dictionary** for help when you aren't sure whether a noun with a plural form has a singular or plural meaning.

Example

Which word should go in the blank?

> If Kelly is going to the party, Joan and Susan ____ going to the store.

a. Is
b. Are
c. Am
d. Was

Try using each choice in the sentence. Choice A, *is*, forms this sentence: If Kelly is going to the party, Joan and Susan is going to the store. There are two people, Joan and Susan, who are going to the store. This makes the subject of the clause plural. *Is* is a singular verb, meaning it does not agree with the subject and cannot be the answer.

Choice B, *are*, forms this sentence: If Kelly is going to the party, Joan and Susan are going to the store. The subject of the clause is still plural. But *are* is a plural verb! The subject and verb agree, so *are* is the correct answer.

Choice C, *am*, forms this sentence: If Kelly is going to the party, Joan and Susan am going to the store. *Am* is a singular verb, and it is also only used in first person, when the writer or speaker is referring to themself. The subject of the clause is plural, and the sentence is in third person, so *am* is not the correct answer.

Choice D, *was*, forms this sentence: If Kelly is going to the party, Joan and Susan was going to the store. *Was* is a singular verb, so it does not agree with the plural subject in this clause.

Complements

A complement is a noun, pronoun, or adjective that is used to give more information about the subject or verb in the sentence.

Direct Objects

A direct object is a noun or pronoun that takes or receives the **action** of a verb. A complete sentence does not need a direct object, so not all sentences will have them. When you are looking for a direct object, find the verb and ask *who* or *what*.

Examples:

> I took *the blanket.*
>
> Jane read *books.*

Indirect Objects

An indirect object is a word or group of words that show how an action had an **influence** on someone or something. If there is an indirect object in a sentence, then you always have a direct object in the sentence. When you are looking for the indirect object, find the verb and ask *to*, *for*, *whom*, or *what.*

Examples:

> We taught [the old dog]_{indirect object} [a new trick]_{direct object}.
>
> I gave [them]_{indirect object} [a math lesson]_{direct object}.

Review Video: Direct and Indirect Objects
Visit mometrix.com/academy and enter code: 817385

Phrases

A phrase is a group of words that functions as a single part of speech, usually a noun, adjective, or adverb. A **phrase** is not a complete thought, and does not contain a subject, but it adds detail or explanation to a sentence, or renames something within the sentence.

Clauses

A clause is a group of words that contains both a subject and a predicate (verb). There are two types of clauses: independent and dependent. An **independent clause** contains a complete thought, while a **dependent (or subordinate) clause** does not. A dependent clause includes a subject and a verb, and may also contain additional information, but it cannot stand as a complete thought without being joined to an independent clause. Dependent clauses function within sentences as adjectives, adverbs, or nouns.

Example:

independent clause: I am running | dependent clause: because I want to stay in shape.

I am running because I want to stay in shape.

The clause *I am running* is an independent clause: it has a subject and a verb, and it gives a complete thought. The clause *because I want to stay in shape* is a dependent clause: it has a subject and a verb, but it does not express a complete thought. This is due to the fact that it begins with *because*, which shows that there is more information needed to complete the thought. This dependent clause adds detail to the independent clause to which it is attached.

> **Review Video: Independent and Dependent Clauses**
> Visit mometrix.com/academy and enter code: 556903

Sentence Structure

Sentence structure is based on the type and number of clauses in the sentence. Two common sentence structures are simple sentences and compound sentences:

Simple

A simple sentence has one independent clause with no dependent clauses. A simple sentence may have a **compound subject** or a **compound verb**, or both.

Examples:

single subject: Judy | single verb: watered

Judy watered the lawn.

compound subject: Judy and Alan | single verb: watered

Judy and Alan watered the lawn.

single subject: Judy | compound verb: watered | compound verb: pulled

Judy watered the lawn and pulled weeds.

compound subject: Judy and Alan | compound verb: watered | compound verb: pulled

Judy and Alan watered the lawn and pulled weeds.

COMPOUND

A compound sentence has two or more independent clauses with no dependent clauses. Usually, the independent clauses are joined with a comma and a coordinating conjunction or with a semicolon.

Examples:

> independent clause — independent clause
> The time has come, and we are ready.

> independent clause — independent clause
> I woke up at dawn ; the sun was just coming up.

COMPLEX

A complex sentence has one independent clause and at least one dependent clause.

Examples:

> dependent clause — independent clause
> Although he had the flu, Harry went to work.

> independent clause — dependent clause
> Marcia got married after she finished college.

Review Video: Sentence Structure
Visit mometrix.com/academy and enter code: 700478

SENTENCE FRAGMENTS

Recall that a group of words must contain at least one **independent clause** in order to be considered a sentence. If it doesn't contain even one independent clause, it is called a **sentence fragment**.

Choosing the best steps for **repairing** a sentence fragment depends on what type of fragment it is. If the fragment is a dependent clause, it can sometimes be fixed by simply removing a subordinating word, such as *when*, *because*, or *if*, from the beginning of the fragment. Alternatively, a dependent clause can be joined to a closely related neighboring sentence. If the fragment is missing some required part, like a subject or a verb, it may be fixed by simply adding the missing part.

Examples:

Fragment: Because he wanted to sail the Mediterranean.

Removed subordinating word: He wanted to sail the Mediterranean.

Combined with another sentence: Because he wanted to sail the Mediterranean, he booked a Greek island cruise.

EXAMPLE

Which of the following changes will NOT correct this sentence fragment?

Although she had found the coin first.

a. Remove *Although*.
b. Add a comma and *she let her brother keep it* after *first*.
c. Add *She let her brother keep the coin* before *although*.
d. Remove *first*.

Choice A suggests removing the word *although* to form the following sentence: She found the coin first. This option removes the subordinating conjunction to make the clause independent. The resulting sentence is complete, so removing *although* is an acceptable way to correct the fragment. Choice A is incorrect.

Choice B forms the following sentence: Although she had found the coin first, she let her brother keep it. A comma and an independent clause have been added to the sentence fragment to form a complex sentence. The resulting sentence is complete and written correctly, so choice B is incorrect.

Choice C forms the following sentence: She let her brother keep the coin although she had found the coin first. An independent clause has been added before the sentence fragment to form a complex sentence. This sentence is correctly written and complete, so choice C is an acceptable way to correct the fragment. Choice C is incorrect.

Choice D removes the word *first*, leaving *Although she had found the coin*. This is still a sentence fragment, since it is a single dependent clause. Choice D does not correct the fragment, so D is correct.

RUN-ON SENTENCES

Run-on sentences consist of multiple independent clauses that have not been joined together properly. Run-on sentences can be corrected in several different ways:

Join clauses properly: This can be done with a comma and coordinating conjunction, with a semicolon, or with a colon or dash if the second clause is explaining something in the first clause.

Example:

> **Incorrect**: I went on the trip, we visited lots of castles.
>
> **Corrected**: I went on the trip, and we visited lots of castles.

Split into separate sentences: This correction is best to use when the independent clauses are very long or when they are not closely related.

Example:

> **Incorrect**: The drive to New York takes ten hours, my uncle lives in Boston.
>
> **Corrected**: The drive to New York takes ten hours. My uncle lives in Boston.

Make one clause dependent: This is the easiest way to make the sentence correct and more interesting at the same time. It's often as simple as adding a subordinating word between the two clauses or before the first clause.

Example:

Incorrect: I finally made it to the store and I bought some eggs.

Corrected: When I finally made it to the store, I bought some eggs.

Reduce to one clause with a compound verb: If both clauses have the same subject, remove the subject from the second clause, and you now have just one clause with a compound verb.

Example:

Incorrect: The drive to New York takes ten hours, it makes me very tired.

Corrected: The drive to New York takes ten hours and makes me very tired.

Note: While these are the simplest ways to correct a run-on sentence, often the best way is to completely reorganize the thoughts in the sentence and rewrite it.

Comma Splices

A comma splice is a specific error that may appear in a run-on sentence. When a sentence has two independent clauses, but the clauses are joined with only a comma, a **comma splice** is formed. Remember that if two independent clauses are joined with a comma, a coordinating conjunction is also needed. Most of the solutions for fixing run-on sentences can also be used to correct a comma splice.

Review Video: Fragments and Run-on Sentences
Visit mometrix.com/academy and enter code: 541989

Example

Rick wants to go see a movie tomorrow he would miss his sister's recital.

Identify the change that would NOT correct this run-on sentence.

a. Add a comma after *tomorrow*.
b. Split it into two sentences between *tomorrow* and *he*.
c. Add a comma and *but* after *tomorrow*.
d. Add a subordinating conjunction to make one of the clauses dependent.

Choice A says to add a comma after *tomorrow*. This forms the following sentence: Rick wants to go see a movie tomorrow, he would miss his sister's recital. A comma has been used to join two independent clauses, but there is no coordinating conjunction. This choice forms a comma splice, so it is not an acceptable correction for this sentence. Choice A is the correct answer.

Choice B says to split the sentence into two sentences. This forms the following two sentences: Rick wants to go see a movie tomorrow. He would miss his sister's recital. Both of these sentences are complete. This is an acceptable way to correct the run-on sentence, so choice B is incorrect.

Choice C says to add a coordinating conjunction after *tomorrow*. This forms the following sentence: Rick wants to go see a movie tomorrow, but he would miss his sister's recital. A comma and a coordinating conjunction have been added between the two independent clauses. This is an acceptable way to correct a run-on sentence. Choice C is incorrect.

Choice D says to add a subordinating conjunction to make one of the sentences dependent. There are many new sentences that could be created by adding a subordinating conjunction. For example, consider the following sentence: Although Rick wants to go see a movie tomorrow, he would miss his sister's recital. Alternatively, the following sentence could also be created: Rick wants to go see a movie tomorrow even though he would miss his sister's recital. Both of these sentences have an independent clause and a dependent clause. These sentences are both complete and written correctly, so choice D is incorrect.

Example

Identify the sentence that has a comma splice.

a. Tom stopped at the store to buy supplies and his family met him at the campsite.
b. The ball rolled into the living room quietly, but it still startled the dog.
c. Theresa brought her mom some flowers, her mom did not have a vase.
d. Sweet potatoes, pecans, and brown sugar are all ingredients in my cousin's sweet potato casserole.

Choice A has two independent clauses joined by a coordinating conjunction. This is incorrect because there should be a comma before the coordinating conjunction. While the sentence is written incorrectly, there is no comma, so this sentence does not have a comma splice. Choice A is incorrect.

Choice B has two independent clauses joined by a comma and a coordinating conjunction. This is the correct way to write a compound sentence, so there is no error here. Choice B is incorrect.

Choice C has two independent clauses joined by a comma. This is incorrect because independent clauses should be joined together by a comma and a coordinating conjunction. When the comma is present without a coordinating conjunction between two independent clauses, a comma splice is formed. This means that choice C is correct.

Choice D is a simple sentence that contains one independent clause. The only commas used in this sentence are used to separate items in a list. There are no clauses that need to be joined or errors related to commas, so choice D does not contain a comma splice. Choice D is incorrect.

Parts of Speech

Nouns

When you talk about a person, place, thing, or idea, you are talking about a **noun**. The two main types of nouns are **common** and **proper** nouns.

Common Nouns

Common nouns are generic names for people, places, and things. Common nouns are not usually capitalized.

Examples of common nouns:

People: boy, girl, worker, manager

Places: school, bank, library, home

Things: dog, cat, truck, car

Proper Nouns

Proper nouns name specific people, places, or things. All proper nouns are capitalized.

Examples of proper nouns:

People: Abraham Lincoln, George Washington, Martin Luther King, Jr.

Places: Los Angeles, California; New York; Asia

Things: Statue of Liberty, Earth, Lincoln Memorial

Note: When referring to the planet that we live on, capitalize *Earth*. When referring to the dirt, rocks, or land, lowercase *earth*.

Singular and Plural Nouns

Singular nouns name **one** person, place, thing, or idea. **Plural nouns** name **more than one** person, place, thing, or idea. Most nouns have both a singular and plural form. Many plural nouns are spelled like the singular noun with an *-s* at the end, but this is not true for all plural nouns. Singular nouns that already end in an *s*, *o*, *ch*, *sh*, or *x* usually end in *-es* when they are in the plural form. Singular nouns that end in a consonant followed by the letter *y* will usually lose the *y* and end in *-ies* in the plural form, and words that end with the letter *f* or *fe* will usually lose the *f* and end in *-ves*.

Some plural nouns have much different spellings than their singular form, and some plural nouns are spelled the same as their singular form. There are more rules for spelling plural nouns, but these are the most common spelling changes.

Examples of singular nouns:

Typical nouns: dog, pencil, girl, store, hope, stingray

Nouns ending in *s*, *o*, *ch*, *sh*, or *x*: mass, hero, lunch, polish, fox

Nouns ending in a consonant and *y*: puppy, baby, fairy, sky

Nouns ending in *f* or *fe*: self, life, calf, hoof

Examples of plural nouns:

Typical nouns: dogs, pencils, girls, stores, hopes, stingrays

Nouns ending in *s*, *o*, *ch*, *sh*, or *x*: masses, heroes, lunches, polishes, foxes

Nouns ending in a consonant and *y*: puppies, babies, fairies, skies

Nouns ending in a vowel and *f* or *fe*: selves, lives, calves, hooves

Collective Nouns

Collective nouns are the names for a group of people, places, or things that function like singular nouns. The following are examples of collective nouns: *class, company, dozen, group, herd, team,* and *public.* Collective nouns usually require an article, such as *a*, *an*, and *the*, which shows that the noun is a single unit. For example, a choir is a group of singers. Even though there are many singers in a choir, the word choir describes a single group. If we refer to the members of the group, and not the group itself, it is no longer a collective noun.

Incorrect: The *choir are* going to compete nationally this year.

Correct: The *choir is* going to compete nationally this year.

Incorrect: The *members* of the choir *is* competing nationally this year.

Correct: The *members* of the choir *are* competing nationally this year.

Pronouns

Pronouns are words that are used to stand in for nouns. There are several different types of pronouns, but the two main types are subjective and objective pronouns. **Subjective** nouns and pronouns that those that are the subject of a sentence. **Objective** nouns and pronouns are those that are an object in a sentence. Another important type of pronoun is the personal pronoun, which refers to people. Personal pronouns can be subjective or objective. **Possessive** nouns and pronouns show possession or ownership. Pronouns can also be singular or plural.

Singular

Subjective	Objective	Possessive
I	Me	My, Mine
You	You	Your, Yours
He	Him	His
She	Her	Her, hers
It	It	Its
Who	Whom	Whose

Plural

Subjective	Objective	Possessive
we	us	our, ours
you	you	your, yours
they	them	their, theirs

Reflexive: Reflexive pronouns are pronouns that function as the object of a sentence and refer to the subject. Examples of reflexive pronouns include *myself, yourself, himself, herself, itself, ourselves, yourselves*, and *themselves.*

Indefinite: Indefinite pronouns are used to refer to multiple nouns or an undefined noun. Examples of indefinite nouns include *all, any, each, everyone, either/neither, one, some*, and *several.*

Relative: Relative pronouns are used to connect relative clauses that specify or describe a noun to the rest of the sentence. Examples of relative pronouns include *which*, *who*, *whom*, and *whose*.

Review Video: Nouns and Pronouns
Visit mometrix.com/academy and enter code: 312073

EXAMPLE

Which of the following sentences uses a relative pronoun?

a. My mother is the person who baked the chocolate cake.
b. Who is in charge of choosing decorations for the party?
c. She is the only person from my hometown to win an Olympic medal.
d. Which car broke down this week?

Remember that a relative pronoun is one that appears at or near the beginning of a relative clause and links the clause to the rest of the sentence. Interrogative pronouns are pronouns that are used to begin a question. Some pronouns, like *who*, *which*, *whom*, and *whose*, can be either interrogative or relative pronouns, depending on how they are used in a sentence, so it is important to pay attention how these words are used in each answer choice.

What is the pronoun in choice A? This sentence includes the word *who*, which can be a relative pronoun. What function does this pronoun have in the sentence? The sentence begins with *my mother is the person*. Which person? *Who* links the relative clause, *who baked the chocolate cake*, to this independent clause and specifies which person the speaker's mother is. That means that *who* is a relative pronoun in this sentence, and choice A is correct.

What is the pronoun in choice B? The first word is *who*, which we know can be a relative pronoun. However, in this sentence, *who* is the first word. It signals the beginning of a question. It does not connect a relative clause to the rest of the sentence. *Who* is an interrogative pronoun in this sentence, so choice B is incorrect.

What is the pronoun in choice C? There is only one pronoun, *my*, which cannot be a relative pronoun. While this sentence could easily be rewritten to include a relative pronoun and clause, it does not include either. Choice C is incorrect.

What is the pronoun in choice D? The first word is *which*, which can be used as either an interrogative or a relative pronoun. *Which* is the first word in this sentence, though. It is not used to link a relative clause that describes or specifies a noun. *Which* is used as an interrogative pronoun in this sentence, so choice D is incorrect.

VERBS

If you want to write a sentence, then you need a verb. Without a verb, you have no sentence. The verb of a sentence indicates action or being. In other words, the verb shows something's action or state of being or the action that has been done to something.

ACTION VERBS AND LINKING VERBS

Action verbs show what the subject is doing. In other words, an action verb shows action. **Linking verbs** link the subject of a sentence to a noun or pronoun. They can also link a subject to an adjective, so the linking verb helps create a description. You always need a verb if you want a complete sentence. However, linking verbs on their own cannot be a complete sentence. Any verb that shows a condition and connects to a noun, pronoun, or adjective that describes the subject of a sentence is a linking verb.

Action: He sings. | Run! | Go! | I talk with him every day. | She reads.

Linking:

Incorrect: I am.

Correct: I am John. | The roses smell lovely. | I feel tired.

Review Video: Action Verbs and Linking Verbs
Visit mometrix.com/academy and enter code: 743142

Verb Tenses

A verb **tense** shows the different form of a verb to point to the time of an action. The present and past tense are indicated by the verb's form. An action in the present, *I talk,* can change form for the past: *I talked*. However, for future tense, an auxiliary, or helping, verb is sometimes needed to show the change in form. When writing a composition, it is important to use verb tenses consistently. Choose the best tense for the composition and do not switch to a different tense unless it is necessary or appropriate for a particular sentence or paragraph.

Present: I talk
Past: I talked
Future: I will talk

Present: The action happens at the current time.

Example: He *walks* to the store every morning.

Past: The action happened in the past.

Example: He *walked* to the store an hour ago.

Future: The action is going to happen later.

Example: I *will walk* to the store tomorrow.

Review Video: Verb Tenses
Visit mometrix.com/academy and enter code: 269472

Irregular Verbs

While most verbs gain the suffix -ed when used in the past tense, irregular verbs receive different spelling changes when they are written in the past tense. For example, *walk* is a regular verb, and it becomes *walked* when written in the past tense. However, *run* is an irregular verb because it becomes *ran* when written in the past tense.

EXAMPLE

My mother _____ me about the big nest of ants near the sandbox. I thanked her for telling me!

Which of the following verbs should go in the blank?

a. Warn
b. Warned
c. Will warn
d. Warns

First, look at the sentences. The first sentence does not have enough information to show which tense it is in. However, the second sentence says that the child thanked the mother. The verb here is *thanked*, which is the past-tense form of *thank*. Because the second sentence is in the past tense, it makes sense to say that the first sentence is also in past tense.

Choice A says that the missing verb is *warn. Warn* is a present-tense verb, but it can be used in the future tense if a helping verb is present. However, this sentence is in past tense, so it needs a past-tense verb. Choice A is wrong.

Choice B says that the missing verb is *warned. Warned* is a past-tense verb, and it logically completes the sentence. Choice B is correct!

Choice C says that the missing verb is *will warn. Will warn* is a future-tense verb, meaning that it describes an action that will occur in the future. However, since the speaker already thanked his or her mother for the warning, it is not logical to use a future-tense verb in the blank. Choice C is incorrect.

Choice D says that the missing verb is *warns. Warn* is usually used with plural subjects, and *warns* used with single subjects. *Warns* can be used in the future or present tense, but it cannot be used in the past tense. Since the sentence is in the past tense, it needs a past-tense verb, so D is incorrect.

ADJECTIVES

An **adjective** is a word that is used to modify a noun or pronoun. An adjective answers a question: *Which one? What kind?* or *How many?* Usually, adjectives come before the words that they modify, but they may also come after a linking verb.

Which one? The *third* suit is my favorite.

What kind? This suit is *navy blue.*

How many? I am going to buy *four* pairs of socks to match the suit.

Review Video: Descriptive Text
Visit mometrix.com/academy and enter code: 174903

COMPARISON WITH ADJECTIVES

Some adjectives are relative, and other adjectives are absolute. Adjectives that are **relative** can show the comparison between things. **Absolute** adjectives can also show comparison, but they do so in a different way. Let's say that you are reading two books. You think that one book is perfect, and the other book is not exactly perfect. It is not possible for one book to be more perfect than the other. Either you think that the book is perfect, or you think that the book is imperfect. In this case, perfect and imperfect are absolute adjectives.

Relative adjectives will show the different **degrees** of something or someone to something else or someone else. The three degrees of adjectives include positive, comparative, and superlative.

The **positive** degree is the normal form of an adjective.

Example: This work is *difficult.* | She is *smart.*

The **comparative** degree compares one person or thing to another person or thing.

Example: This work is *more difficult* than your work. | She is *smarter* than me.

The **superlative** degree compares more than two people or things.

Example: This is the *most difficult* work of my life. | She is the *smartest* lady in school.

Review Video: Adjectives
Visit mometrix.com/academy and enter code: 470154

Adverbs

An **adverb** is a word that is used to **modify,** or describe, a verb, adjective, or another adverb. Usually, adverbs answer one of these questions: *When? Where? How?* and *Why?* The negatives *not* and *never* are considered adverbs. Adverbs that modify adjectives or other adverbs **strengthen** or **weaken** the words that they modify.

Examples:

He walks *quickly* through the crowd.

The water flows *smoothly* on the rocks.

Note: Adverbs are usually indicated by the suffix *-ly*, which has been added to the root word. For instance, *quick* can be made into an adverb by adding *-ly* to construct *quickly*. Some words that end in *-ly* do not follow this rule and can function as other parts of speech. Examples of adjectives ending in *-ly* include: *early, friendly, holy, lonely, silly*, and *ugly*. To know if a word that ends in *-ly* is an adjective or adverb, check your dictionary. Also, while many adverbs end in *-ly*, you need to remember that not all adverbs end in *-ly*.

Examples:

He is *never* angry.

You are *too* irresponsible to travel alone.

Types of Adverbs

Different types of adverbs are used to describe particular aspects of a verb, adjective, or other adverb. The following are examples of common types of adverbs:

Time: Some adverbs show when something was done, such as *yesterday, today*, or *in two days.*

Manner: Some adverbs show the way something was done, such as *hurriedly, neatly, grumpily*, or *loudly.*

Frequency: Some adverbs show how often something was done, such as *seldom*, *often*, *never*, or *often*.

Degree: Some adverbs show how much or to what degree something was done, such as *completely*, *barely*, *highly*, or *halfway*.

Conjunctive: Conjunctive adverbs are used similarly to conjunctions, as they connect different ideas, but they can connect ideas from different clauses or sentences. Some examples of conjunctive adverbs are *however*, *alternatively*, *likewise*, and *then*.

COMPARISON WITH ADVERBS

The rules for comparing adverbs are the same as the rules for adjectives.

The **positive** degree is the standard form of an adverb.

> Example: He arrives *soon*. | She speaks *softly* to her friends.

The **comparative** degree compares one person or thing to another person or thing.

> Example: He arrives *sooner* than Sarah. | She speaks *more softly* than him.

The **superlative** degree compares more than two people or things.

> Example: He arrives *soonest* of the group. | She speaks the *most softly* of any of her friends.

Review Video: Adverbs
Visit mometrix.com/academy and enter code: 713951

EXAMPLE

Identify the conjunctive adverb in the following sentences.

> Every night, Savannah's brother loudly gets up to get a glass of water. Consequently, she has started sleeping with earmuffs on so that he does not wake her up at night.

a. Every night
b. Loudly
c. Consequently
d. At night

Choice A says that *every night* is a conjunctive adverb. What does *every night* describe in this sentence? It describes how often Savannah's brother loudly gets a glass of water. This means that *every night* shows the frequency that Savannah's brother does this action. Since *every night* is an adverb that shows frequency, choice A is incorrect.

Choice B says that *loudly* is a conjunctive adverb. In this sentence, what does *loudly* describe? It describes the way that Savannah's brother gets a glass of water each night. This means that *loudly* is an adverb that shows manner. *Loudly* is not a conjunctive adverb, so choice B is incorrect.

Choice C says that *consequently* is a conjunctive adverb. What function does *consequently* have in this sentence? It shows the reason that Savannah started wearing earmuffs while she sleeps. It also shows a connection between the information in the first sentence and the information in the second sentence. Since *consequently* connects the ideas in these sentences, it is a conjunctive adverb. Choice C is correct.

Choice D says that *at night* is a conjunctive adverb. *At* and *night* work together to form an adverbial phrase. Which type of adverb do they form? In this sentence, *at night* shows when Savannah wants to avoid being woken up by her brother. This makes *at night* an adverb that shows time, meaning that *at night* is not a conjunctive adverb and choice D is incorrect.

Prepositions

A **preposition** is a word placed before a noun or pronoun that shows the relationship between an object and another word in the sentence.

Common prepositions:

about	before	during	on	under
after	beneath	for	over	until
against	between	from	past	up
among	beyond	in	through	with
around	by	of	to	within
at	down	off	toward	without

Examples:

> The napkin is *in* the drawer.
>
> The Earth rotates *around* the Sun.
>
> The needle is *beneath* the haystack.
>
> Can you find "me" *among* the words?

Prepositional Phrases

One important thing to know about prepositions is that they form special phrases, called prepositional phrases. A **prepositional phrase** begins with a preposition and ends with a noun or pronoun that is the object of the preposition. Normally, the prepositional phrase functions as an **adjective** or an **adverb** within the sentence.

Examples:

> prepositional phrase: on the blanket
>
> The picnic is on the blanket.
>
> prepositional phrase: with a fever
>
> I am sick with a fever today.
>
> prepositional phrase: Among the many flowers
>
> Among the many flowers, John found a four-leaf clover.

Be careful not to mistake the object in a prepositional phrase as the subject of a sentence. The subject of the sentence will not be found in a prepositional phrase because a prepositional phrase is used to describe how an object is related to the subject. Prepositional phrases do not influence subject-verb agreement.

Prepositional phrases do not influence subject-verb agreement. For example, consider the following sentence:

The basket (simple subject) of clothes (prepositional phrase) is (verb) on the floor in the laundry room.

This sentence contains a prepositional phrase between the simple subject and the verb. The simple subject is *basket*, which is a singular noun, and the verb is *is*, which is a singular verb. They are separated by the prepositional phrase "of clothes." Even though the plural noun *clothes* comes right before the singular verb *is*, this verb shows the action of the singular noun *basket*.

Review Video: Prepositions
Visit mometrix.com/academy and enter code: 946763

Example

Which of the following could NOT complete the sentence?

She went ____ the cave.

a. Sadly
b. Into
c. From
d. Through

Choice A says that the missing word is *sadly*. The blank is between *went* and *the cave*, meaning that the missing word will connect these pieces of the sentence. While *sadly* could be used here to show how the girl felt, there would still be missing information. A preposition is needed here to show whether she entered, exited, or stood outside of the cave. *Sadly* is an adverb, so A is the correct answer.

Choice B says that *into* would complete the sentence. Does *into* complete the sentence without leaving missing information? To say *she went into the cave* is a logical, complete sentence. Choice B is incorrect.

Choice C says that the missing word is *from*. This creates the sentence *she went from the cave*. Since she could have left the cave to go somewhere else, this is also a logical, complete sentence. Choice C is incorrect.

Choice D says that *through* would complete the sentence. The sentence would read *she went through the cave*. Since she could have explored the whole cave or found an exit on the other side of it, *through* can logically complete the sentence. Choice D is incorrect.

Example

Identify the prepositional phrase in the following sentence.

Mable visited the store to buy some vegetables.

a. To buy
b. Visited the store
c. The store to buy
d. To buy some vegetables

Remember the pieces of a prepositional phrase. Prepositional phrases should begin with a preposition and end with a noun or pronoun. Considering these rules, can any of the answer choices be eliminated? Choice B and choice C can be eliminated because neither choice begins with a preposition!

That leaves choices A and D. Choice A says that the prepositional phrase is *to buy*. This does start with a preposition, and it does give more information about Mable's trip to the store. However, it does not end with a noun or pronoun. Choice D says that the prepositional phrase is *to buy some vegetables*. Choice D begins with a preposition and ends with a noun, and it explains why Mabel went to the store.

Choice D is the only choice that has all of the pieces of a prepositional phrase, so D is correct!

Example

Read the sentence below and answer the following question.

> A band with 15 members _____ performing at my restaurant tonight.

Identify the verb that best completes the sentence.

a. Were
b. Is
c. Are
d. Are not

This question is asking which verb should go in the blank. There are a couple of reasons why choosing the correct verb for this sentence may be confusing. First of all, there are two nouns that appear before the verb. Second, one of these nouns is singular and one is plural.

The first step is to determine which noun goes with the verb. The two nouns are *band* and *members*. While *members* is closest to the blank, it is part of a prepositional phrase that describes *band*. The subject of the sentence is *band*, so the verb must agree with *band*.

Is *band* singular or plural? The sentence says that the band has multiple members, but there is only one band. *Band* is a collective noun, meaning that it is a singular noun. This means that the correct verb will also be singular. With this in mind, can any of the answer choices be eliminated?

Choices A, C, and D are all plural verbs. Even though the blank appears after a plural noun, this noun is part of a prepositional phrase. The verb should match the singular subject *band*. The only choice with a singular verb is choice B, so B is the correct answer.

Conjunctions

Conjunctions join words, phrases, or clauses and they show the connection between the joined pieces. **Coordinating conjunctions** connect equal parts of sentences. Coordinating conjunctions can also be used to create compound subjects and compound predicates, in addition to compound sentences.

Coordinating Conjunctions

The **coordinating conjunctions** include: *and, but, yet, or, nor, for,* and *so*

Compound Subjects:

compound subject
Terry *and* Marissa went to the movies last Saturday.

compund subject
Either pumpkin pie *or* apple pie would be a good dessert to bring to Thanksgiving dinner.

compound subject
Neither the clownfish *nor* the goldfish liked the new fish food very much.

Compound Predicates:

compound predicate
Veronica left school *and* picked up her sister from soccer practice.

compound predicate
The cat did not take a nap *or* play with the dog yesterday.

Compound Sentences:

The rock was small, *but* it was heavy.

She drove in the night, *and* he drove in the day.

Bill dressed nicely today, *for* he must give an important presentation this afternoon.

Correlative Conjunctions

Some examples of **correlative conjunctions** are: *either...or* | *neither...nor* | *not only...but also*. When one correlative conjunction is used, its matching correlative conjunction will be used later in the sentence.

Examples:

Either you are coming *or* you are staying.

He *not only* ran three miles *but also* swam 200 yards.

Review Video: Coordinating and Correlative Conjunctions
Visit mometrix.com/academy and enter code: 390329

Subordinating Conjunctions

Subordinating conjunctions link dependent clauses, clauses with either a subject or a predicate, to independent clauses, clauses with both a subject and a predicate, to form a complex sentence. The subordinating conjunction will always be at the beginning of the dependent clause. When the dependent clause is at the beginning of the sentence, it will end with a comma. When the independent clause is at the beginning of the sentence, no comma is needed.

Common **subordinating conjunctions** include:

after	since	whenever
although	so that	where
because	unless	wherever
before	until	whether
in order that	when	while

Examples:

I am hungry *because* I did not eat breakfast.

He went home *when* everyone left.

While her brother ate dinner, she played his favorite video game.

Review Video: Subordinating Conjunctions
Visit mometrix.com/academy and enter code: 958913

Example

Which of the following is a complex sentence?

a. Joseph went grocery shopping and put all of the groceries away at home.
b. Joseph went grocery shopping, and he put all of the groceries away at home.
c. Joseph went grocery shopping and put all of the groceries away when he got home.
d. Joseph went grocery shopping; he put all of the groceries away at home.

Choice A contains one subject and a compound predicate. Because there is only one subject, Joseph, there is only one clause. Since the sentence is made of one independent clause and a prepositional phrase, it is a simple sentence, and choice A is incorrect.

Choice B contains two clauses. The clauses are separated by a comma and a coordinating conjunction, and both are independent clauses. This sentence contains a prepositional phrase and two independent clauses, so it is a compound sentence. Choice B is incorrect.

Choice C contains two clauses. There are two subjects in the sentence, *Joseph* and *he*. Even though one clause is much shorter than the other, these subjects each go with a different clause. The first clause is independent. The second clause is dependent, as it begins with the word *when*. Since the sentence is made of one independent clause and one dependent clause, it is a complex sentence. Choice C is correct.

Choice D contains two clauses. They are both independent clauses, because they both contain a subject and a predicate, and they both form complete thoughts. Since there is no coordinating conjunction, they are linked by a semicolon. Since the sentence is made from two independent clauses, it is a compound sentence. Choice D is incorrect.

Example

Identify the sentence that contains correlative conjunctions.

a. She can wait for her friend's letter to arrive, or she can call her now.
b. He must leave now, or he will end up in heavy traffic when he gets on the highway.
c. When your grandfather gets here, you can greet him with a handshake or a hug.
d. I can't decide whether to go to my brother's concert or to study for my test tomorrow.

Read the answer choices carefully. Remember that correlative conjunctions appear in pairs, so there will be at least two conjunctions in the sentence. Additionally, these conjunctions will go together. The information given immediately after the first conjunction will make little sense without the information that comes after the second conjunction.

Choice A contains the conjunction *or*. Though *or* can be a correlative conjunction, in this sentence, it is used by itself to connect two independent clauses. This means it is a coordinating conjunction. There are no correlative conjunctions in this sentence, so choice A is incorrect.

Choice B contains the conjunctions *or* and *when*. Again, *or* can be a correlative conjunction. However, the sentence could end after *traffic*. The information beginning with *when* is not needed to complete the thought, and *or* and *when* do not form a pair of correlative conjunctions. Choice B is incorrect.

Choice C contains the conjunctions *when* and *or*. *When* is used to begin a dependent clause. *Or* is used to form a compound object by linking *handshake* and *hug*. These conjunctions do not work together in this sentence, so they are not correlative conjunctions. Choice C is incorrect.

Choice D contains the conjunctions *whether* and *or*. *Whether* is used to introduce one choice the speaker can make, and *or* is used to introduce an alternative choice. If the sentence ended before *or*, it would be an incomplete thought. The conjunctions *whether* and *or* go together in this sentence, and they are correlative conjunctions. Choice D is correct.

End Punctuation

Periods

Use a period to end all sentences except direct questions and exclamations. Periods are also used for abbreviations.

Examples: 3 p.m. | 2 a.m. | Mr. Jones | Mrs. Stevens | Dr. Smith | Bill, Jr. | Pennsylvania Ave.

Note: An abbreviation is a shortened form of a word or phrase.

Question Marks

Question marks should be used following a **direct question**. A polite request can be followed by a period instead of a question mark.

Direct Question: What is for lunch today? | How are you? | Why is that the answer?

Polite Requests: Can you please send me the item tomorrow. | Will you please walk with me on the track.

Review Video: Question Marks
Visit mometrix.com/academy and enter code: 118471

Exclamation Marks

Exclamation marks are used after a word group or sentence that shows much feeling or has special importance. Exclamation marks should not be overused. They are saved for proper **exclamatory interjections**.

Example: We're going to the finals! | You have a beautiful car! | "That's crazy!" she yelled.

Review Video: Exclamation Points
Visit mometrix.com/academy and enter code: 199367

Commas

The comma is a punctuation mark that can help you understand connections in a sentence. Not every sentence needs a comma. However, if a sentence needs a comma, you need to put it in the right place. A comma in the wrong place or a missing comma will make a sentence's meaning unclear. These are some of the rules for commas:

Use Case	Example
Before a **coordinating conjunction** joining independent clauses in compound sentences	Bob caught three fish, and I caught two fish.
Between **items in a series**	I will bring the turkey, the pie, and the coffee.
After a **dependent clause** that **begins a complex sentence**	Before she left, Ashley turned off all of the lights in her house.
After **transition words**	Consequently, Joel's mother grounded him.
After an **introductory phrase**	After the final out, we went to a restaurant to celebrate.
After a **prepositional phrase** at the **beginning of a sentence**	After a **prepositional phrase** at the **beginning of a sentence**

Review Video: When To Use a Comma
Visit mometrix.com/academy and enter code: 786797

Example

Which of the following sentences is NOT missing a comma?

a. During a play you should be quiet and respect the performers.
b. I finally fell asleep after my father turned the television off.
c. Until she finishes her vegetables she must stay at the table.
d. At the third stop sign take a right.

Remember that there are several reasons a comma may be needed in a sentence. After an introductory phrase, a transition, or a dependent clause at the beginning of a sentence are some of the most common places that a comma is needed.

Choice A is a simple sentence that begins with a prepositional phrase. Is a comma needed? Prepositional phrases can be introductory phrases, so a comma should follow them when they appear at the beginning of a sentence. The prepositional phrase in this sentence, *during a play*, functions as an introductory phrase and should be followed by a comma. Choice A is incorrect.

Choice B is a complex sentence. Are commas needed in complex sentences? When the dependent clause comes first, a comma should be used at the end of that clause. In choice B, the first clause is independent and the second is dependent. This means that no comma is needed, so the sentence is not missing any punctuation marks. Choice B is correct.

Choice C is a complex sentence. The sentence begins with *until*, which is a subordinating conjunction. This shows that the sentence begins with a dependent clause. This is a complex sentence, so the dependent clause should be followed by a comma. A comma is missing after *vegetables*, so choice C is incorrect.

Choice D is a simple sentence. Like choice A, this sentence begins with a prepositional phrase. *At the third stop sign* functions as an introductory phrase, so it should be followed by a comma. Choice D is incorrect.

EXAMPLE

Where should a comma be added in the following sentence?

Though the mountain is very steep he is not afraid to scale it.

a. After *Though*
b. After *mountain*
c. After *steep*
d. After *afraid*

Choice A says there should be a comma after *though*. In this sentence, *though* is a subordinating conjunction that begins a dependent clause. Remember that a comma goes at the end of a dependent clause that appears at the beginning of a sentence. *Though* is at the beginning of the clause, and there is no other need for a comma right after it. Choice A is incorrect.

Choice B says there should be a comma after *mountain*. *Mountain* is the subject of the dependent clause in this sentence. The comma should go at the end of the dependent clause. *Mountain* appears in the middle of the dependent clause, not at the end of it. Choice B is incorrect.

Choice C says there should be a comma after *steep*. *Steep* is the last word in the dependent clause that begins the sentence. Adding a comma here would correctly separate the dependent clause from the following independent clause. This is the correct place for the comma, so choice C is correct.

Choice D says there should be a comma after *afraid*. *Afraid* is the verb in the independent clause, and there is no need to separate it from the rest of the sentence. Choice D is incorrect.

EXAMPLE

Where should a comma be added in the following sentence?

However she forgot to turn the water off before she walked away from the sink.

a. After *However*
b. After *forgot*
c. After *off*
d. After *away*

Choice A says there should be a comma after *however*. *However* is a transition word that appears at the beginning of the sentence. Transitions are separated from the rest of the sentence by commas, so adding a comma after *however* is correct. Choice A is the correct answer.

Choice B says there should be a comma after *forgot*. In this sentence, *forgot* is in the middle of an independent clause. There is no reason for a comma after *forgot*, so choice B is incorrect.

Choice C says there should be a comma after *off*. This is a complex sentence, meaning it contains an independent clause and a dependent clause. While *off* is the last word in the independent clause, remember that a comma is not needed to separate clauses in a complex sentence unless the dependent clause comes first. Since the independent clause is first in this sentence, no comma is needed after *off*. Choice C is incorrect.

Choice D says there should be a comma after *away*. *Away* appears in the middle of a dependent clause, so its location in the sentence does not call for a comma. *Away* is not part of a list, transition, or introductory phrase, either. There is no need for a comma here, so choice D is incorrect.

QUOTATION MARKS

Use quotation marks to close off **direct quotations** of a person's written or spoken words, which are also called **dialogue**. Do not use quotation marks around indirect quotations. An indirect quotation gives someone's message without using the person's exact words. Use **single quotation marks** to close off a quotation inside a quotation.

> **Direct Quote**: Nancy said, "I am waiting for Henry to arrive."
>
> **Indirect Quote**: Henry said that he is going to be late to the meeting.
>
> **Quote inside a Quote**: The teacher asked, "Has everyone read Martin Luther King's 'I Have a Dream' speech?"

Quotation marks should be used around the titles of **short works**: newspaper and magazine articles, poems, short stories, songs, television episodes, and radio programs. Titles of **long works** should be italicized when they are part of a typed composition or underlined when they are part of a handwritten composition.

Examples:

> "Rip Van Winkle" (short story by Washington Irving)
>
> "O Captain! My Captain!" (poem by Walt Whitman)

Review Video: Quotation Marks
Visit mometrix.com/academy and enter code: 884918

Apostrophes

An apostrophe is used to show **possession** or the **deletion of letters in contractions**. An apostrophe is not needed with the possessive pronouns *his, hers, its, ours, theirs, whose*, and *yours*.

Singular Nouns: David's car | a book's theme | my brother's board game

Plural Nouns that end with -*s*: the scissors' handle | boys' basketball

Plural Nouns that end without -*s*: Men's department | the people's adventure

Review Video: Apostrophes
Visit mometrix.com/academy and enter code: 213068

Review Video: Punctuation Errors in Possessive Pronouns
Visit mometrix.com/academy and enter code: 221438

Apostrophes in Contractions

Contractions are combinations of words. Contractions involve taking two words, removing at least one letter from one of the words, putting an apostrophe in its place, and removing the space. For example, *does not* can be written as the contraction *doesn't*. The *o* is removed from *not* and is replaced with an apostrophe, which represents the removed letter, so it appears as *n't*. The space after does is then removed, turning *does not* into the contraction *doesn't*. Some more examples of contractions are listed below.

First Word	Second Word	Contraction
Can	Not	Can't
Do	Not	Don't
She	Will	She'll
They	Will	They'll
He	Is	He's
It	Is	It's
They	Are	They're
I	Am	I'm

Not all words can be used to form contractions, but many small, commonly used words can.

Capitalization

One important part of using correct grammar is properly capitalizing words. Usually, only nouns will be capitalized, but there are some exceptions. The most important capitalization rule is that the first word of every sentence, no matter what part of speech it is, should be capitalized. Another exception is that the pronoun *I* should always be capitalized.

Proper nouns are always capitalized, but sometimes it can be tricky to decide whether or not a noun is a proper noun. Some words that are usually common nouns may become proper nouns when used with other words or phrases. Also, when words that are not nouns are used with a noun, or when a group of words are used together as one noun, those words may also need to be capitalized.

Titles of Books, Stories, and Essays

Most of the words in titles of things like books, stories, and essays should be capitalized, but some should not. The very first word in a title should always be capitalized. Any other word in a title that is a noun, pronoun, adjective, verb or adverb should be capitalized. Articles, such as *a* or *the*, should not be capitalized. Short conjunctions and prepositions are usually not capitalized.

Abbreviations, Initials, and Acronyms

Abbreviations are shortened versions of other words. When an abbreviation shortens, or abbreviates, a word that should be capitalized, the abbreviation's first letter should also be capitalized. When the shortened word is a noun that is not capitalized, the abbreviation should be in lowercase. Initials are usually written using the first letter from multiple words. For example, John Fitzgerald Kennedy is commonly referred to by his initials, JFK. Acronyms also use the first letter from multiple words, but they are different from initials because they form words on their own. For example, NASA is an acronym for National Aeronautics and Space Administration. Some acronyms, like NASA, omit small words, such as *and*, *of*, and *for*. When initials and acronyms are used for proper nouns, each letter should be capitalized.

The types of words and phrases in the chart below are proper nouns and should always be capitalized:

	Description	**Example**
Historical Periods	A range of time in history that is related to specific events or circumstances	During the Romantic Period, many authors and poets wrote about their emotions.
Historical Events	Names of important events that happened in history	Napoleon Bonaparte led France after the French Revolution.
Historical Documents	Titles of important papers or compositions that are connected to historical events	The Mayflower Compact was written to create rules and expectations for the colony in Plymouth.
Languages	Names of the different languages that people speak	I want to learn to speak Cantonese, Spanish, and German.
Races and Ethnicities	Words often used to describe a person's heritage or cultural group	Malia taught her granddaughter how to hula so she could share a tradition of her Native Hawaiian heritage with her.
Nationalities	Words that describe which country a person is from	My teacher who moved to Canada last year is Romanian.

	Description	Example
Organizations	Titles of official groups formed by people	Fewer than half of the states in America have a team in the National Basketball Association.

Review Video: Capitalization in Grammar
Visit mometrix.com/academy and enter code: 369678

EXAMPLE

Choose the correctly capitalized organization name.

a. National Association for People who Hate Taking Naps
b. Organization for The Most Interesting People in America
c. Club for High-School Students Who love Reading
d. Nebraskan Club for Mountain Climbers

Names of organizations follow the same capitalization rules as titles. Remember that when capitalizing titles, it is important to consider each word's part of speech. Nouns, pronouns, verbs, adjectives, and adverbs are always capitalized in titles. Consider the part of speech of every word in each answer choice.

In choice A, the capitalized words include adjectives, nouns, and verbs. These words are all correctly capitalized. *For* and *who* are in lowercase. Which parts of speech are these words? *For* is a preposition. Remember that short prepositions are not usually capitalized in titles, so leaving *for* in lowercase is acceptable. *Who* is a pronoun. Pronouns should always be capitalized in titles, so this is an error. Choice A is incorrect.

In choice B, there is an incorrectly capitalized word. An article should not be capitalized in a title unless it is the first word in the title. In this choice, *the* is capitalized in the middle of the title. This is an error, so choice B is incorrect.

In choice C, each capitalized word is correct. These words include nouns, adjectives, a pronoun, and a verb. *For* and *love* are in lowercase. Since *for* is a short preposition, it is acceptable to leave it in lowercase. However, *love* is a verb in this title. Verbs must be capitalized in titles, so this is an error. Choice C is incorrect.

In choice D, the capitalized words include adjectives and nouns. Words belonging to these parts of speech should always be capitalized in titles. The only word that is in lowercase is *for*, which may be left in lowercase because it is a short preposition. All of the words in this organization name are correctly capitalized or left in lowercase, so choice D is correct!

Example

Identify the capitalization mistake in the following sentences.

> My brother and I want to open a bakery, so we discussed what we should call it. I wanted to give it a name that would form the acronym Bake, but we couldn't think of a good name using those letters. My brother suggested Bakery Brothers and said that if we ever need to abbreviate the name, we can call it Bakery Bros. or BB.

a. All of the letters in *Bake* should be capitalized.
b. *Bakery Brothers* should be in lowercase.
c. All of the letters in *Bros.* should be capitalized.
d. The second *B* in *BB* should be lowercase.

There are three types of abbreviations in these sentences. The second sentence contains an acronym, and the third sentence contains a shortened word and an initialism. Consider the different capitalization rules for each of these to identify the error in the sentences.

Choice A says that all of the letters in *Bake* should be capitalized. Even though *bake* is a verb that usually should not be capitalized at all, it is used as an acronym in this sentence. That means that each letter should be capitalized, so choice A is correct.

Choice B says that all of the letters in *Bakery Brothers* should be in lowercase. In the sentences, *Bakery Brothers* is the full name of the bakery. Since it is the name of a place, *Bakery Brothers* is a proper noun. It is correctly capitalized, so choice B is incorrect.

Choice C says that all of the letters in *Bros.* should be capitalized. *Bros.* is a shortening of *brothers.* Remember that shortened words should follow the same capitalization rules as the original word. Since the first letter of *brothers* is capitalized in the phrase *Bakery Brothers*, *Bros.* is written correctly. Choice C is incorrect.

Choice D says that the second *B* in *BB* should be in lowercase. *BB* is an initialism that takes the first letter from each word in the name *Bakery Brothers*. Remember that all of the letters in initialisms must be capitalized, so *BB* is correctly capitalized. Choice D is incorrect.

Word Confusion

To, Too, and Two

To can be an adverb or a preposition for showing direction, purpose, and relationship. A dictionary can also be used to see the many other ways to use *to* in a sentence.

> Examples: I went to the store. | I want to go with you.

Too is an adverb that means *also, as well, very,* or *in excess.*

> Examples: I can walk a mile too. | You have eaten too much.

Two is a number.

> Example: You have two minutes left.

THERE, THEIR, AND THEY'RE

There can be an adjective, adverb, or pronoun. Often, *there* is used to show a place or to start a sentence.

> Examples: I went there yesterday. | There is something in his pocket.

Their is a pronoun that is used to show ownership.

> Examples: He is their father. | This is their fourth apology this week.

They're is a contraction of *they are*.

> Example: Did you know that they're in town?

ITS AND IT'S

Its is a possessive pronoun that shows ownership.

> Example: The guitar is in its case.

It's is a contraction of *it is*.

> Example: It's an honor and a privilege to meet you.

AFFECT AND EFFECT

There are two main reasons that *affect* and *effect* are so often confused: 1) both words can be used as either a noun or a verb, and 2) unlike most homophones, their usage and meanings are closely related to each other. Here is a quick explanation of the four usage options:

Affect (n): feeling, emotion, or mood that is displayed

> Example: The patient had a flat *affect*. (i.e., his face showed little or no emotion)

Affect (v): to alter, to change, to influence

> Example: The sunshine *affects* the plant's growth.

Effect (n): a result, a consequence

> Example: What *effect* will this weather have on our schedule?

Effect (v): to bring about, to cause to be

> Example: These new rules will *effect* order in the office.

EXAMPLE

Choose the correct spelling from each pair of homophones in the following passage.

> I found a unique tree in the forest. (It's/Its) trunk is blue, and it has (two/too) many branches to count. I brought some of my friends to see it, but the tree did not seem to (affect/effect) them. While (their/they're) not fascinated by the strange tree, I am!

The first pair of homophones is *it's* and *its*. Remember that the contraction *it's* is used in place of *it is*. *Its* is a possessive pronoun that shows a thing's ownership or possession. An easy way to decide whether *it's* or *its* is correct is to see how the sentence sounds with *it is*, instead. *It is trunk is blue* does not make sense. *Its trunk is blue* means that the tree has a blue trunk, so *its* is the correct choice.

The next pair of homophones is *two* and *too*. *Two* only means the number two. *Too* can mean *also* or *in excess*. Which of these makes the most sense in this sentence? *Two many branches to count* or *too many branches to count*? The correct meaning is that there is an abundance of branches, so *too* is the correct choice for this pair.

The third pair of homophones is *affect* and *effect*. Since both of these words can be used as a noun or verb, identifying the correct part of speech is a helpful first step. The part of speech is a verb, since the correct word will show what *the tree* does to *them*. *Affect* as a verb means to change or influence. *Effect* as a verb means to lead to or cause something to happen. Replace the homophone with these synonyms. Seeing the tree cannot cause or lead the speaker's friends to exist, but it can change them or influence them. *Affect* is the correct choice for this pair.

The last pair of homophones is *their* and *they're*. *Their* is a possessive pronoun used to show that multiple people or things own something. *They're* is a contraction used in place of *they are*. Replace the homophone with *they are*. Does the sentence make sense? It does because they, the speaker's friends, are not fascinated by the tree. Saying *their not fascinated* does not make sense. *They're* is the correct choice for this pair.

Chapter Quiz

1. Every sentence always has a subject and a/an:

a. Imperative
b. Preposition
c. Predicate
d. Modifier

2. Which of the following sentences does NOT have an implied subject?

a. Take John on a quick walk.
b. Don't get lost.
c. John knows the way to the park.
d. Bring me back some flowers.

3. Which pronoun can be either singular or plural depending on what it is representing in the context of the sentence?

a. Nobody
b. Either
c. Several
d. All

4. Which of the following is written in third person perspective?

a. I am walking
b. He is walking
c. You are walking
d. We are walking

5. Which of the following best describes the function of an indirect object?

a. Shows how an action had an influence
b. Takes or receives the action of a verb
c. Explains or describes the subject
d. Shows that there is more information needed

6. Which of the following is a group of words that contains both a subject and a verb, and can be either independent or dependent?

a. Antecedent
b. Fragment
c. Phrase
d. Clause

7. Which of the following is an example of a complex sentence (as opposed to a simple or compound sentence)?

a. The time has come, and we are ready.
b. Judy and Alan watered the lawn and pulled weeds.
c. Marcia got married after she finished college.
d. I woke up at dawn; the sun was just coming up.

8. What method of correcting run-on sentences is the easiest way to make the sentence correct and more interesting at the same time?

a. Split into separate sentences
b. Join clauses properly
c. Reduce to one clause with a compound verb
d. Make one clause dependent

9. Which of the following is a word placed before a noun or pronoun that shows the relationship between an object and another word in the sentence?

a. Adjective
b. Adverb
c. Preposition
d. Conjunction

10. Which of the following should be put in single quotation marks?

a. Quote inside a quote
b. Indirect quote
c. Direct quote
d. All of the above

Chapter Quiz Answer Key

1. C: See section **Predicates**

2. C: See section **Subjects**

3. D: See section **Depend on Context**

4. B: See section **Person Agreement Examples**

5. A: See section **Indirect Objects**

6. D: See section **Clauses**

7. C: See section **Complex**

8. D: See section **Run-on Sentences**

9. C: See section **Prepositions**

10. A: See section **Quotation Marks**

Extended Constructed Response

Essays

Essays usually focus on one topic, subject, or goal. There are several types of essays, including informative, persuasive, and narrative. An essay's structure and formality depend on the type of essay and its goal. While narrative essays typically do not include outside sources, other types of essays often require some research and the use of primary and secondary sources.

The basic format of an essay typically has three major parts: the introduction, the body, and the conclusion. The body is further divided into the writer's main points. Most essays will have at least three main points, but essays that go into more depth can have almost any number of main points.

An essay's introduction should answer three questions:

1. What is the **subject** of the essay?

   If an essay is about a book, the answer would include the title and author of the book, as well as any additional information needed, such as the subject or argument of the book.

2. How does the essay **discuss** the subject?

   To answer this, the writer briefly summarizes the main points and the evidence supporting them to let readers know how the essay is organized and what information they can expect to read.

3. What will the essay **prove**?

   This information is in the thesis statement, usually the opening paragraph's last sentence, which clearly states the writer's message.

The body elaborates on all the main points related to the thesis, introducing one main point at a time, and includes supporting evidence with each main point. Each body paragraph should state the point in a topic sentence, which is usually the first sentence in the paragraph. The paragraph should then explain the point's meaning, support it with quotations or other evidence, and then explain how this point and the evidence are related to the thesis. The writer should then repeat this procedure in a new paragraph for each additional main point.

The conclusion restates the content of the introduction, including the thesis, to remind the reader of the essay's main argument or subject. The essay writer may also summarize the highlights of the argument or description contained in the body of the essay, following the same organization originally used in the body. For example, a conclusion might look like: Point 1 + Point 2 + Point 3 = Thesis, or Point 1 → Point 2 → Point 3 → Thesis Proof. Good organization makes essays easier for writers to compose and provides a guide for readers to follow. Well-organized essays hold attention better and are more likely to get readers to believe or agree with the writer.

Using Sources in Essays

Sometimes writers use information from others in their work. This is most common in expository and persuasive writing. For an expository essay, a writer may not know all of the information that he or she needs to finish the composition. The writer may use other people's work to find the missing information and complete the composition. Persuasive writers may do research to find facts or statements from others that support their own beliefs and make their writing more persuasive. In both cases, research helps the writer find information that **supports** his or her **original work**.

Outside information must be relevant, true, and helpful to be appropriate for a composition. Writers must also be careful not to use too much outside information, since this can make the composition unoriginal. If a writer does use outside information, it is extremely important that the writer mention in the composition where the information came from. If the writer forgets or chooses not to say where the information came from, he or she has stolen someone else's work and presented it as their own. Doing this is called **plagiarism**.

Informational Texts

Informational texts, also called instructional or expository texts, are compositions written to inform the reader about a specific topic. An informational essay can inform readers in a variety of ways, such as giving them instructions, telling them facts about the topic, or teaching them why something happens. Informational texts should be logical, meaning that they should present information in an order that the reader can easily understand, and they should include the right amount of information so the writer successfully informs his or her audience of new information.

Informational texts should also focus on a **controlling idea**. In the introduction of an informational text, there may be a sentence or two that clearly state the essay's controlling idea. This sentence, or sentences, is called a **thesis statement**. The controlling idea should be clear throughout the composition. By emphasizing the controlling idea in the introduction, body, and conclusion, the writer can ensure that the controlling idea is clear. One way to make sure that the controlling idea is emphasized is to think about the purpose of each part of the essay. The introduction prepares the reader by telling them what the rest of the essay is about, so the controlling idea should be **introduced** in this section. The body tells the reader the information the writer wants to tell the audience, so this **explains** the controlling idea and facts about it to the reader. The conclusion is used to **remind** the reader of how the information in the body is related and **restates** the controlling idea one final time.

Review Video: Informational Text
Visit mometrix.com/academy and enter code: 924964

Structures or Organizational Patterns in Informational Texts

Informational text can be **descriptive**, meaning that it gives information that can be experienced through the five senses, or it answers the questions what, who, when, where, and why. One common method of organizing informational text is to put it in a certain sequence, or order. **Chronological** texts include events in the order that they occurred, from start to finish. **How-to**, or **instructional**, texts organize information into a series of instructions in the order in which the steps should be followed. **Comparison-contrast** structures of informational text describe different ideas to their readers by pointing out how things or ideas are similar and how they are different.

Cause and effect structures of informational text describe events that occurred and the causes or reasons for those events. **Problem and solution** structures of informational texts introduce and describe problems and offer one or more solutions for each problem described.

ARGUMENTATIVE WRITING

In argumentative writing, the writer expresses a belief or opinion that he or she wants to lead readers to agree with. When writing an argumentative composition, the writer should first identify the **topic** his or her opinion is about. The topic may be serious or fun, as long as there is one clear topic in the composition. The next step is for the writer to determine his or her opinion on the topic and determine why he or she holds that opinion. In order to persuade others to agree with their opinion, the writer must be able to give readers reasons to support the opinion. If the writer does not know why he or she has an opinion, it will be difficult to convince readers to agree. In addition to having reasons that support their opinion, writers should prepare examples that support each of these reasons in order to strengthen their composition.

Once the writer has determined his or her topic, opinion, and reasons for having the opinion, he or she is ready to begin writing an argumentative essay. In the introduction, the writer should capture the reader's interest, introduce the topic, and reveal his or her opinion about the topic. In the body of the composition, the writer should remind the reader of the opinion and give his or her reasons for holding the opinion. If the writer has any examples, facts, or other information that supports his or her opinion or reasons for believing it, these should also be included in the body. Writers may also use a body paragraph to mention opposing opinions or beliefs and explain why they disagree with them. As in other compositions, the conclusion should remind the reader of the essay's topic and purpose, as well as remind the reader how the opinion has been explained and supported. The conclusion should also invite the reader to continue thinking about the topic and writer's opinion. This can be done through questions or statements that lead readers to consider whether or not they agree with the author's opinion or what their own opinions are.

Review Video: Argumentative Writing
Visit mometrix.com/academy and enter code: 561544

INFORMATIVE VS. PERSUASIVE WRITING

Informative writing, also called explanatory or expository writing, is written to show that something is true or factual, while **persuasive** writing is written to lead the reader to agree with something that may or may not be true or factual. While persuasive text is written to **persuade** readers to agree with the author's position, informative text simply **provides information** to readers. Informative writing **informs** readers about why or how something is as it is. This can include offering new information, explaining how a process works, or describing a concept for readers.

FACTS AND OPINIONS

Writers and readers must always be aware of the difference between fact and opinion. A **fact** can be tested and proven to be true. An **opinion**, on the other hand, is someone's personal thoughts or feelings. Opinions are often not changed by information. If an author writes that a newborn elephant is about five times taller than a newborn giraffe, then he or she is stating a fact. If the author writes that giraffes are more interesting than elephants, then he or she is giving an opinion because this cannot be proven to be true or false. Opinions are often supported by facts. For instance, the author might use a comparison between the way that giraffes eat and the way elephants eat as evidence of how giraffes are more interesting. An opinion supported by facts tends to be more convincing. On the other hand, when authors support their opinions with other opinions, readers should seriously think about and read the argument carefully to see whether it is logical and trustworthy.

> **Review Video: Distinguishing Fact and Opinion**
> Visit mometrix.com/academy and enter code: 870899

Responding to a Text

An essay prompt may require writers to write about a text they have read. When writing an essay like this, writers should show that they understand the text they have read. They may mention their own thoughts, ideas, and opinions in the essay. However, the main idea of the essay should be about the text mentioned in the prompt.

When planning the essay, writers should consider what the text is about and how it is written. Writers should identify the purpose, main idea, and structure of the text. For informational and persuasive texts, they should also think about the supporting details the author used in the text. All of these facts about the text will help writers understand the text well and allow the writer to create a response to the text.

Responding to Multiple Texts

Essay prompts may ask writers to write about more than one text. In this case, writers should identify the purpose, main idea, and structure of each text. They should also look at the kinds of supporting details that the author of each text uses. Once writers know these details, they should think about the differences and similarities between the texts. The main ideas of each text may oppose each other, or one may support the other. Writers will need to write about both texts in the essay, so they must understand both texts and the connection between the texts.

Correspondence

Letters are written using a different format than an essay or book. A letter should begin with a greeting that names the person or group that is meant to receive the letter. Consider the following examples of greetings:

- Dear Mr. Johnson,
- To whom it may concern:
- To Bernard,
- Hello Grandma,

The greeting used at the beginning of the letter depends on the writer's purpose for writing the letter. If the letter is being written to a business, an owner or manager of a company, or someone who has a higher rank than the writer, the letter should be **formal**. A formal greeting should begin with "Dear" followed by the name of the recipient. For formal greetings, never address the recipient by their first name only. If the letter is being written to a friend or a family member, it may be **informal**. For informal letters, the greeting may start with a word other than *dear* and may name the recipient by their first name only or by a nickname.

Word Choice and Tone in Letters

The **purpose** of a letter also influences the way the body of the letter is written. For formal letters, the writer should use **formal, professional language**. The purpose of the letter should be clearly stated in the introduction. Whether the letter is written to give a complaint or share an opinion, the writer should keep a formal tone and write in a way that is **respectful** to the recipient. The writer should also be specific and provide any information that the recipient may need to respond appropriately. If a letter is informal, the writer can use **casual, friendly language**. The writer should think about their own relationship with the recipient and use a tone that fits the relationship and purpose for the letter.

Closing Letters

All letters should end with a **closing**, as well. The closing will include a word or phrase that signals that the body of the letter has ended, such as *sincerely*, *best wishes*, *until later*, or *with love*. The word or phrase should be followed by a comma, and the writer's name should be written underneath this on the next line. Formal letters should include closing words like *sincerely* or *thank you*.

Chapter Quiz

1. What type of essay does NOT typically include outside sources?

a. Expository
b. Informative
c. Persuasive
d. Narrative

2. Which of the following is NOT true of informational texts?

a. Informational texts are also called instructional or expository texts
b. Informational texts should be logical
c. Informational texts should focus on a central idea
d. Informational texts can only be structured chronologically

3. In an argumentative essay, which of the following should be included in the body?

a. A reminder of the writer's opinion and his or her reasons for holding the opinion
b. Examples, facts, or other information that supports the writer's opinion
c. Opposing opinions or beliefs and explanations of why the writer disagrees with them
d. All of the above

4. A letter that requires a formal greeting should always start with:

a. Dear
b. To whom it may concern
c. Greetings
d. Hello

5. At the end of a letter the closing is followed by:

a. A period and the writer's name
b. A comma and the writer's name
c. A colon and the writer's name
d. A semicolon and the writer's name

Chapter Quiz Answer Key

1. D: See section **Essays**

2. D: See section **Structures or Organizational Patterns in Informational Texts**

3. D: See section **Argumentative Writing**

4. A: See section **Correspondence**

5. B: See section **Closing Letters**

Informational Text Example

Below is a prompt for an informational text. There is also an example of an essay that addresses the prompt. There are multiple drafts of this essay to show what kinds of changes a writer may make during the writing process to improve his or her work.

Prompt:

One of the things that makes each person unique is the hobbies they enjoy doing in their free time. Write about a hobby you enjoy. Be sure to include information about how you became interested in the hobby.

Rough Draft

Prepare to see your boredom disappear before your very eyes! Presto! That is what my favorite hobby did for me. Learning and performing magic tricks for my friends and family is my favorite hobby.

Every time we go to my grandparents' house, he does a card trick when we get there. Last year on my birthday, he gave me a cool deck of cards and showed me how to do a trick. I practiced it a couple of times and then tried it with some of my friends. I did it correctly with most of them, and they were so impressed! I was looking up new card tricks online when I discovered that there are other kinds of magic tricks, too. I decided to learn one to show my grandpa the next time he visited. I ended up learning five tricks that day! Since then, learning magic tricks has been my hobby.

Before I started learning magic tricks, my hobby was collecting rocks. I started collecting rocks around my neighborhood, but then I also started collecting them on vacations. I enjoyed that hobby until school started again. Then I had fewer opportunities to find cool rocks. I enjoy learning magic tricks much more, and it is something I can do any day after school. I also like learning magic tricks more that collecting things because it is more exciting. Looking at the rocks I had collected got old, but I never get tired of magic tricks!

One of my favorite things about my hobby is that I can perform magic shows. Once I have learned several new magic tricks, I get to do a magic show for my parents and my sister. If there was ever a talent show at school, I would do magic tricks as my talent. It is fun to show off the tricks I have learned, but my favorite part of doing magic shows is seeing that others enjoy my magic tricks. I love that I can share my hobby with others!

I am very thankful to my grandpa for inspiring my hobby! I believe I will always love doing magic tricks and hope I can become a better magician if I keep learning and practicing!

Revised Draft

Prepare to see your boredom disappear before your very eyes! Presto! That is what my favorite hobby did for me. Learning and performing magic tricks for my friends and family is my favorite hobby.

Every time we go to my grandparents' house, he does a card trick when we get there. Last year on my birthday, he gave me a cool deck of cards and showed me how to do a trick. I practiced it a couple of times and then tried it with some of my friends. I did it correctly with most of them, and they were so impressed! I was looking up new card tricks online when I discovered that there are other kinds of magic tricks, too. I decided to learn one to show my grandpa the next time he visited. I ended up learning five tricks that day! Since then, learning magic tricks has been my hobby.

~~Before I started learning magic tricks, my hobby was collecting rocks. I started collecting rocks around my neighborhood, but then I also started collecting them on vacations. I enjoyed that hobby until school started again. Then I had fewer opportunities to find cool rocks. I enjoy learning magic tricks much more, and it is something I can do any day after school. I also like learning magic tricks more that collecting things because it is more exciting. Looking at the rocks I had collected got old, but I never get tired of magic tricks!~~

One of my favorite things about my hobby is that I can perform magic shows. Once I have learned several new magic tricks, I get to do a magic show for my parents and my sister. If there was ever a talent show at school, I would do magic tricks as my talent. It is fun to show off the tricks I have learned, but my favorite part of doing magic shows is seeing that others enjoy my magic tricks. I love that I can share my hobby with others!

I still enjoy watching others do magic tricks, but I enjoy learning and performing them even more. I am very thankful to my grandpa for inspiring my hobby! I believe I will always love doing magic tricks and hope I can become a better magician if I keep learning and practicing!

Revised Draft Notes

Remember the purpose of the revising stage of the writing process. When revising, it is important to look at the whole composition. Do all of the paragraphs strengthen the composition? Do the introduction and conclusion help the reader understand the controlling idea and main points?

First, look at the underlined words. These are words that have been added. In the conclusion, a sentence has been added. This sentence strengthens the composition because it creates a transition from the body to the conclusion. It also gives the writer's thoughts about the details he or she included in the essay. Before, the conclusion began abruptly and only mentioned one of the writer's points from the body of the composition. After this sentence was added, the conclusion became about each of the writer's points from the body paragraphs. This sentence reminds the reader of the writer's points and the composition's controlling idea, instead of focusing on only one of the writer's points.

Next, look at what has been crossed out in this essay. These are words that have been removed. A whole paragraph has been omitted! Why is that? There were no huge errors, and the writing made sense. The paragraph talks about why learning magic tricks is better than the writer's former hobby. While this is related to the controlling idea, this information is not entirely relevant and does not offer much new information about magic tricks. This paragraph does not strengthen the composition or help the reader understand the controlling idea. The writer made a wise choice to remove this information and should later replace it with a paragraph that gives the reader new information about the writer's hobby, why the writer enjoys it, or something the writer has experienced through it.

Edited Draft

Prepare to see your boredom disappear before your very eyes! Presto! ~~That is what my favorite hobby did for me.~~ Learning and performing magic tricks for my friends and family is my favorite hobby.

My interest in magic tricks was inspired by my grandpa. Every time we go to my grandparents' house, he does a card trick when we get there. Last year on my birthday, he gave me a cool deck of cards and showed me how to do a trick. I practiced it a couple of times and then tried it with some of my friends. I did it correctly with most of them, and they were so impressed! I was looking up new card tricks online when I discovered that there are other kinds of magic tricks, too. I decided to learn one to show my grandpa the next time he visited. I ended up learning five tricks that day! Since then, learning magic tricks has been my hobby.

~~Before I started learning magic tricks, my hobby was collecting rocks. I started collecting rocks around my neighborhood, but then I also started collecting them on vacations. I enjoyed that hobby until school started again. Then I had fewer opportunities to find cool rocks. I enjoy learning magic tricks much more, and it is something I can do any day after school. I also like learning magic tricks more that collecting things because it is more exciting. Looking at the rocks I had collected got old, but I never get tired of magic tricks!~~

One of my favorite things about my hobby is that I can perform magic shows. Once I have learned several new magic tricks, I get to do a magic show for my parents and my sister. ~~If there was ever a talent show at school, I would do magic tricks as my talent.~~ My sister wants me to do a magic show at her birthday party. I am so excited to do my magic tricks for a new audience! It is fun to show off the tricks I have learned, but my favorite part of doing magic shows is seeing that others enjoy my magic tricks. I love that I can share my hobby with others!

I still enjoy watching others do magic tricks, but I enjoy learning and performing them even more. I am very thankful to my grandpa for inspiring my hobby! I believe I will always love doing magic tricks and hope I can become a better magician if I keep learning and practicing!

Edited Draft Notes

Since the writer has revised his or her work, the next step is to edit the composition. Remember that editing is very similar to revising, but editing usually includes paying attention to each paragraph, instead of the whole composition. Look at the changes that were made to each paragraph.

In the introduction, a sentence was removed. Why was it removed? While it said something about hobbies, it did not strengthen the composition. This sentence connects the hook to the prompt, but it does not introduce the topic or give the reader useful information. This sentence is not about the specific hobby being discussed in the composition. While it gives a transition from the hook to the thesis, a different sentence would better prepare the reader for the information in the rest of the essay.

Only one change has been made in the second paragraph. A transition has been added to the beginning of the first sentence. This helps connect this paragraph to the rest of the composition and prepares the reader for the information in the paragraph. Before, this paragraph simply described an event and explained how it led the writer to begin his or her hobby. However, the reader is not told why the paragraph is relevant until later in the paragraph. Now, the reader is told the purpose at the beginning of the paragraph. This strengthens the composition by improving how this paragraph flows with the rest of the essay.

What has been changed in the fourth paragraph? Another sentence has been crossed out, and two new ones have been added. Why? This paragraph tells why the writer enjoys doing magic shows, and it includes the example of magic shows the writer has performed for his or her family. The end of the paragraph tells the reasons why the writer has enjoyed doing the magic shows. The crossed-out sentence tells the reader that the author would do a magic act for a school talent show. This detail is relevant to the rest of the paragraph, but it does not support the paragraph's main point. The underlined sentences include supporting details that explain that the writer has an opportunity to do a show for a new audience. This example is better because it elaborates on the first example and connects the examples to the reason the writer enjoys doing magic shows. These sentences help the paragraph flow better and support the other ideas in the paragraph.

The remaining marks are left to remind the writer that the third paragraph still needs to be replaced. This information will be added before the final draft is finished.

FINAL DRAFT

Prepare to see your boredom disappear before your very eyes! Presto! That is what happened to me when I began learning how to do magic tricks. Now, learning and performing magic tricks for my friends and family is my favorite hobby.

My interest in magic tricks was inspired by my grandpa. Every time we go to my grandparents' house, he does a card trick when we get there. Last year on my birthday, he gave me a cool deck of cards and showed me how to do a trick. I practiced it a couple of times and then tried it with some of my friends. I did it correctly with most of them, and they were so impressed! I was looking up new card tricks online when I discovered that there are other kinds of magic tricks, too. I decided to learn one to show my grandpa the next time he visited. I ended up learning five tricks that day! Since then, magic tricks have been my hobby.

While doing magic tricks is very fun, it takes practice at first. Some tricks are difficult to get the hang of because you have to do some steps very carefully. For example, for some tricks, you have to hide a small object in your hand or behind your hand. If the object is not completely hidden or if you make it too obvious that you are hiding something, the trick does not work as well. These tricks are very difficult for me to learn, so I have to practice them more than other tricks. Sometimes it takes patience, but mastering a trick is so fun that practicing is worth it!

One of my favorite things about my hobby is that I can perform magic shows. Once I have learned several new magic tricks, I get to do a magic show for my parents and my sister. My sister wants me to do a magic show at her birthday party. I am so excited to do my magic tricks for a new audience! It is fun to show off the tricks I have learned, but my favorite part of doing magic shows is seeing that others enjoy my magic tricks. I love that I can share my hobby with others!

I still enjoy watching others do magic tricks, but I enjoy learning and performing them even more. I am very thankful to my grandpa for inspiring my hobby! I believe I will always love doing magic tricks and hope I can become a better magician if I keep learning and practicing!

Final Draft Notes

This is the final draft! In this draft, information has been added to the introduction, and there is a new paragraph. Now, the introduction includes a sentence that introduces the controlling idea of the composition and prepares the reader for the information in the rest of the essay. The new paragraph also gives new information about doing magic tricks. This paragraph describes a lesson the writer learned through doing magic tricks and gives the reader more information about the writer's experience practicing the hobby. These additions strengthen the composition by replacing weaker information with details that are more informative and engaging for the reader.

Evaluation

The essay answers the prompt and is on topic throughout the composition. The controlling idea is clear and is stated in the introduction, supported in the body, and restated in the conclusion. The thesis statement restates parts of the prompt and gives the reader a preview of the rest of the essay. The body uses well-structured paragraphs to explain the supporting details and examples and connects them to the controlling idea. The conclusion also emphasizes the controlling idea and supporting details and invites the reader to consider what they have read.

The essay is also interesting and written with a variety of sentence types. It uses transitions and good paragraph structure to make the essay easy for the reader to understand. The introduction also uses a hook to get the reader's attention and help him or her relate to the information in the essay. Not only does this essay answer the prompt and have appropriate structure, but it also makes use of good, engaging, and interesting details.

Practice Test #1

Reading

Fog

Stealthy fog drifts through the air,
A dense, gray blanket everywhere.
It slowly seeps in from the sea,
Clutching rooftops, climbing trees.

Its eerie whisper fills the land—
"Catch me, catch me, if you can!"
It skims the sky and hugs the ground,
Distorts the vision, muffles sound.

It fills the mind and fools the feet
Like haunting shadows in the street.
It creeps across the alleyway
And dims the newborn light of day.

It smothers landscapes without shame
Then fades as quickly as it came.

Refer to the passage "Fog" to answer questions 1-7.

1. What is the meaning of the word *distorts*, used in line 8?

a. Quiets
b. Sharpens
c. Changes
d. Stops

2. How does the poet use the metaphor in line 2 to describe a characteristic of the fog?

a. To show that fog can disappear like a ghost
b. To show that fog speaks like a person
c. To show that fog can be like a heavy covering
d. To show that fog can move like an animal

3. Based on lines 13 and 14, which of the following is most likely true about fog?

a. Fog can be dangerous
b. Only places near the water get fog
c. Fog is expected to happen every day
d. The effects of fog are temporary

4. Based on the theme of *Fog*, which of the following titles would be best for this poem?

a. Fog, the Mysterious Traveler
b. Dark Day on an Island
c. Types of Cloudy Weather
d. The Science Behind Fog

5. What does the poet show by ending "Fog" with two lines instead of four?

a. How boring fog can be
b. How quickly fog disappears
c. How thin fog really is
d. How much fog wants to leave

6. Which phrase from the poem shows that fog can make it difficult to see things?

a. Clutching rooftops, climbing trees
b. It fills the mind and fools the feet
c. Its eerie whisper fills the land
d. Distorts the vision, muffles sound

7. How does the poet's personification of fog in lines 5 and 6 affect the mood of the poem?

a. It describes the fleeting nature of fog and creates a mysterious mood
b. It describes the darkness of fog and creates a sad mood
c. It describes the friendly nature of fog and creates a hopeful mood
d. It describes the danger of fog and creates a warning mood

Geocaching

(1) "Would you like to go geocaching with me this weekend, Tommy?" asked his father. "I have found a couple of new ones near the creek that I think would be fun. We could invite your friend Sam to join us."

(2) "Sure, Dad. I love geocaching," said Tommy. "Should we go on Saturday?" They agreed that they would leave Saturday morning to find the new geocaches, and Tommy ran to call Sam and invite him. Sam agreed to come with them. Although he wasn't sure what geocaching was, he always had fun with Tommy and his dad.

(3) Friday night, Tommy and his dad got their gear ready. They both had handheld GPS units, hiking boots with good wool socks, a backpack to carry first aid gear, water, and swag for the cache such as plastic soldiers, a water pistol, and some playing cards. Tommy's father made sure that they had a compass, a map, bug spray, and hats, and he printed out the coordinates for the geocaches. Tommy had given Sam a list of things to bring with him as well.

(4) Saturday morning, Tommy and Dad picked up Sam at his house, and off they went. "Mr. Jones, could you explain to me what geocaching is?" Sam asked as they were getting in the car.

(5) "Of course, Sam. Basically, it's like a giant worldwide treasure hunt. People hide geocaches, or containers, then take the coordinates with their GPS and enter the coordinates into a website where people like us can find them. Then, other people, like us, go hunting for these containers. Some of them are very tiny, just big enough to have a piece of paper for the date and your name. Some of them are large enough to hold books or toys and a logbook. Sometimes people even put disposable cameras in them so you can take a picture of yourself at the cache. There are even items in some caches that can be tracked so you can see how they move around the world."

(6) Tommy's dad could see that Sam was still a little confused, but he knew that the boy would catch on as they got going. Mr. Jones put the coordinates for the first cache into his GPS, and they headed off. "It looks like this first cache is only two miles from here," he told the boys.

(7) The GPS led the trio to a small parking area just inside the local park, where they stopped and got their backpacks on. They also sprayed themselves with bug spray and reset the GPS for off-road walking. "It looks like we have about 400 feet to go just that way," Mr. Jones said as they headed away from the car into the woods. When they arrived at the location, Sam looked around. "I don't see anything," he complained.

(8) Tommy laughed. "Our GPS is accurate to 15 feet, Sam, which means that the cache container is within 15 feet of Dad right now but in any direction. The way we do it is Dad stands still, and I walk 15 feet from him. Then we know how far in each direction to look. Why don't I walk 15 feet to his right and you go left? Then we know exactly where to search." Sam agreed, and the boys quickly marked off their search area. "The cache is medium sized, Sam, so be looking for something like the plastic boxes your mom puts leftovers in, okay?"

(9) Tommy, Sam, and Mr. Jones searched for about 10 minutes. They looked in tree branches, under rocks and leaves, and even inside a hollow log before Sam yelled, "I think I found it!" Sure enough, he had found the container under a pile of leaves beside the hollow log. Since this was Sam's first find, Tommy and his dad let Sam open the box and choose an item to trade. Sam chose to take a bouncy rubber ball and leave a water gun. Mr. Jones signed the logbook for all of them, and they hid the cache back where they found it.

(10) "That was so much fun, Tommy! I'm so glad you asked me to come along," Sam said excitedly.

(11) "Does that mean you boys are ready to find the next one?" Mr. Jones asked. The boys cheered, and the three of them set off for the car.

Refer to the passage "Geocaching" to answer questions 8-16.

8. What will most likely happen during Tommy and Sam's next geocache hunt?

a. Tommy will find the next geocache since Sam found this one.
b. Mr. Jones will not need to use his GPS to help locate the geocache.
c. Sam will be upset if someone else finds the geocache.
d. The next geocache will have an item that gets traded.

9. Which event in "Geocaching" marks the climax of the story?

a. When Tommy and his dad pick up Sam
b. When Sam finds the cache under the leaves
c. When Mr. Jones inputs the GPS coordinates
d. When the group sets off to find the next cache

10. This question has two parts. After you answer Part A, answer Part B:

Part A: Based on paragraphs 7 and 8, what conclusion can the reader make about geocaching?

a. Only one cache was hidden in the park where the group searched.
b. All caches are the same size.
c. Caches are most often hidden in parks.
d. Using GPS coordinates may not take someone to the exact location of a cache.

Part B: Which of the following lines from the passage supports the answer to Part A?

a. "Our GPS is accurate to 15 feet, Sam, which means that the cache container is within 15 feet of Dad right now but in any direction."
b. The GPS led the trio to a small parking area just inside the local park, where they stopped and got their backpacks on.
c. "The cache is medium sized, Sam, so be looking for something like the plastic boxes your mom puts leftovers in, okay?"
d. They also sprayed themselves with bug spray and reset the GPS for off-road walking.

11. Which of the following gives the best summary of "Geocaching"?

a. Sam does not want to go geocaching because he does not know how, but Tommy convinces him to try it out. Mr. Jones explains geocaching to Sam on the drive to the park. Once Sam finds the first geocache, he is eager to find more.
b. Tommy invites Sam to go geocaching with him and his dad. Sam is new to geocaching and does not fully understand how it works at first, but he is excited after he finds the first cache. Sam gets to trade items in the cache, and the group sets off for the next one.
c. Tommy and his dad, Mr. Jones, pick up Sam on a Saturday morning for an adventure. Mr. Jones explains geocaching to Sam, who selects a water gun to place in the cache he finds and takes a rubber bouncy ball in return.
d. Sam, Tommy, and Mr. Jones walk through a local park with their backpacks and happen to find a treasure. The treasure was hidden under a pile of leaves by a log. They discover that it is a geocache and decide to try to find another one.

12. At the beginning of the passage, Sam is confused about what geocaching is. He complains that he does not see anything when the group arrives at the GPS coordinates. How do Sam's responses help develop the story's plot?

a. They give Sam a reason to be excited when he is the one to find the cache.
b. They show that Sam is reliant on the help of others when geocaching.
c. They highlight the value of the treasured items that Sam selects for the cache.
d. They explain why Sam has never been geocaching before.

13. Why did Mr. Jones and the boys hide the cache back where they found it in paragraph 9?

a. They did not have room in their packs to take the cache with them.
b. They did not like the treasure that was in the cache.
c. They wanted other geocachers to also have the chance to find the treasure.
d. They wanted to confuse other geocachers.

14. The word *geocaching* uses the prefix *geo-*, which comes from Greek and means *earth*. Based on this information and the passage, what is the meaning of the word *geocache*?

a. A container that is made from natural materials
b. An object that is hidden somewhere outdoors
c. A treasured object that is buried in the earth
d. An object that tells people where they are on Earth

15. Why would the passage "Geocaching" be best described as realistic fiction?

a. The story imagines how a historical event could have happened.
b. The story centers around an unexplained event.
c. The story could happen in real life to real people.
d. The story involves a crime that needs to be solved.

16. What does the third-person omniscient point of view allow the reader to understand?

a. There is a process to follow and gear needed for geocaching.
b. Sam became excited after finding the first cache of the day.
c. Sam was confused before the hunt, and Mr. Jones knew this.
d. It is valuable to use GPS coordinates to locate a cache.

Living on a Ranch

(1) Marcus Morgan lives in Laramie, Wyoming with his family. Laramie is between the Snowy Mountain Range and the Laramie Mountain Range, west of Cheyenne, Wyoming.

(2) Marcus and his family own a large cattle ranch outside of the city along U.S. Route 287. The Bar M Bar Ranch raises both beef and dairy cattle, along with a small herd of sheep. Mrs. Morgan keeps chickens and tends a small garden to feed the family. Marcus and his two brothers, James and Robert, have to help with chores and taking care of the animals.

(3) Life starts early on the ranch. Mrs. Morgan rings the bell to bring everyone in for breakfast at 4:30 am. The family eats breakfast with the ranch hands, and then the boys do their morning chores before heading off to school. When the boys return from school, they have more chores to complete before dinner and homework time.

(4) Everyone has a job on the ranch. Mr. Morgan supervises the ranch hands, oversees repairs, and takes care of all the vehicles on the ranch. Mrs. Morgan is in charge of paying the bills and making sure everyone is fed. Marcus, at 15 years old, is the oldest child and has the most responsibility. He has to let the sheep out every morning and bring them back in every evening. He helps in the milking barn or with branding beef cattle when needed. He also takes care of the working dogs used all over the ranch. James gathers eggs, brings in a fresh pail of milk every morning, and cleans out horse stalls in the evenings. Robert, the baby of the family, helps his mom around the house and in the garden.

(5) Marcus especially likes working with the sheep. In the mornings, he and his favorite working dog, Shep, run the sheep out of their corral into the big pasture so they can graze. Marcus uses whistles and calls to tell Shep where he wants the sheep to go, and Shep herds them. In the evenings, Marcus and Shep round up the sheep from the pasture and return them to the corral. Then, Marcus must feed the sheep and check them for injuries. In the spring, Marcus and Shep help Mr. Morgan bring the sheep into the shearing shed one at a time to have their wool sheared.

Island Ponies

(1) Assateague Island is on the east coast. It is a long, thin island. It is so long that two-thirds of it is in Maryland and one-third in Virginia. The Maryland end of the island contains the majority of the Assateague National Seashore and Assateague Park. The southern end of the island, in Virginia, contains the Chincoteague National Wildlife Refuge.

(2) Two herds of wild ponies live on this island. The ponies that live in Maryland are called the Assateague horses, and the ponies that live in Virginia are called the Chincoteague ponies. Standing only an average of 13.2 hands high, or 54 inches, they are considered ponies because of how short they are. Both herds look alike, too. The ponies can be either solid colored or pinto patterned. The two herds are the same breed of horse, but they are treated very differently.

(3) The Assateague horses are considered wild animals. Unless there is a dire need, they are left alone to survive on the poor habitat available on the Assateague National Seashore. The rangers do not give them veterinarian checkups, teach them to ride, or teach them to enjoy being around humans. They live as they have since the first ponies came to the island after a Spanish galleon sank off the coast in the 1500s.

(4) A veterinarian, however, checks the Chincoteague ponies twice a year. They are given shots that help keep them healthy despite the poor vegetation on the island. The Virginia ponies are used to people because of this treatment. The Chincoteague herd is managed by the Chincoteague Volunteer Fire Department, which holds a very special pony sale every year.

(5) Assateague Island isn't very large, so the herds have to be kept small so they have enough food and room. Both herds average 150 ponies. To keep the Chincoteague herd that small, the Fire Department rounds up the Chincoteague ponies every July by using bigger horses to drive them into the water for the 10-minute swim to Chincoteague Island. Veterinarians check the ponies, and then some of them are sold to spectators who want a pony of their own. The remainder of the herd is allowed to rest, and then they are pushed to swim back to their home island.

(6) The money from this sale helps the Fire Department buy new equipment and pays for the veterinarians who take care of the herd. It also helps to keep people interested in the ponies. So many people come to this sale and love the ponies that there is even a famous children's book about one of the first ponies sold.

Refer to the passage "Living on a Ranch" to answer questions 17-19.

17. Which two conclusions about the ranch are supported by the information in the passage? Select all that may apply.

a. People come to the ranch to buy cattle for beef and dairy.
b. The ranch is a family business.
c. There are more sheep than cattle on the ranch.
d. All the animals on the ranch are used for food.
e. Both people and animals have specific jobs on the ranch.

18. Which sentence best explains the role of the sheep on the Bar M Bar Ranch?

a. The Bar M Bar Ranch raises both beef and dairy cattle, along with a small herd of sheep.
b. He has to let the sheep out every morning and bring them back in every evening.
c. Then, Marcus must feed the sheep and check them for injuries.
d. In the spring, Marcus and Shep help Mr. Morgan bring the sheep into the shearing shed one at a time to have their wool sheared.

19. Which of the following describes the author's purpose for writing "Living on a Ranch"?

a. To explain Marcus' relationship with his brothers
b. To describe the hard work of living on a ranch
c. To argue that cows are the most useful animal on the ranch
d. To highlight the role of the working dogs on the ranch

Refer to the passage "Island Ponies" to answer questions 20-24.

20. Which key idea about the Assateague ponies is supported by paragraph 3?

a. The Assateague ponies are an endangered species.
b. The Assateague ponies are smaller than horses.
c. The Assateague ponies do not have much contact with humans.
d. The Assateague ponies are treated better than the Chincoteague ponies.

21. The author's purpose in the way that they organized the passage "Island Ponies" was most likely to:

a. Highlight the differences in the ways people view the two herds of ponies
b. Describe what it is like to encounter the island ponies when they are treated and sold
c. Use a narrative storyline about the ponies' history to entertain the reader
d. Present a solution to how the Chincoteague pony population should be managed

22. Which of the following ideas about the Chincoteague ponies is supported by paragraphs 4 through 6?

a. People think the Chincoteague ponies are special.
b. Buying a Chincoteague pony is expensive.
c. All of the Chincoteague ponies are always healthy.
d. Chincoteague ponies are not used to being around humans.

23. The main idea of "Island Ponies" is best shown in which sentence?

a. The southern end of the island, in Virginia, has the Chincoteague National Wildlife Refuge.
b. The two herds are the same breed of horse, but they are treated very differently.
c. A veterinarian, however, checks the Chincoteague ponies twice a year.
d. The Assateague horses are considered wild animals.

24. Which of the following describes the organizational pattern the author used in "Island Ponies"?

a. A descriptive pattern to show the step-by-step process veterinarians follow to care for the Chincoteague ponies
b. A cause-and-effect pattern to show how the treatment of the Assateague ponies had caused them to dislike humans
c. A compare-and-contrast pattern to show that the Assateague and Chincoteague ponies are similar but receive different treatment from humans
d. An advantage-and-disadvantage pattern to show the positive and negative effects of buying a Chincoteague pony

Refer to the passages "Living on a Ranch" and "Island Ponies" to answer questions 25-27.

25. How are the animals in "Life on a Ranch" different from the animals in "Island Ponies"?

a. None of the animals in "Life on a Ranch" are sold for money, but all of the animals in "Island Ponies" are.
b. All of the animals in "Life on a Ranch" spend time with humans, but none of the animals in "Island Ponies" do.
c. The animals in "Life on a Ranch" all have a specific purpose in the work of the ranch, but the animals in "Island Ponies" do not have a specific purpose on the island.
d. The animals in "Life on a Ranch" are all used for food, but the animals in "Island Ponies" are not.

26. In what way is the care of the sheep in "Life on a Ranch" similar to the care of the Chincoteague ponies in "Island Ponies"?

a. Both the sheep and the Chincoteague ponies are cared for every day.
b. Both the sheep and the Chincoteague ponies are given special food to eat.
c. Both the sheep and the Chincoteague ponies are usually left alone.
d. Both the sheep and the Chincoteague ponies are checked so they can stay healthy.

27. What is described by both paragraph 5 in "Life on a Ranch" and paragraph 5 in "Island Ponies"?

a. What it's like to own an animal
b. How each animal finds food
c. A yearly event involving the animals
d. Why the animals enjoy being around humans

Extended Response

Your STAAR test will include the following instructions for your extended response question. The response prompts used here are similar to the prompts you will see on the STAAR test.

28. Read the passages "Living on a Ranch" and "Island Ponies." Based on the passages, write a response to the following:

> Explain your opinion about whether animals should or should not be owned by people.

Write a well-organized argumentative composition that uses specific evidence from the passages to support your answer.

Remember to —

- clearly state your controlling idea
- organize your writing
- develop your ideas in detail
- use evidence from the selections in your response
- use correct spelling, capitalization, punctuation, and grammar

Manage your time carefully so that you can —

- review the selection
- plan your response
- write your response
- revise and edit your response

Revising

George wrote the following paper about his trip to the zoo. Read the following paper and note the revisions that George should make. Once you have read his paper, answer the questions that follow it.

A Zany Trip to the Zoo

(1) As the school bus came to a stop, I became more and more excited: the day of the zoo trip had finally arrived! (2) My backpack was packed with a camera, binoculars, my watch, sunglasses, and a hat. (3) The week before, I looked on the zoo's website to see what kind of animals were at the zoo. (4) I discovered that there was a dolphin exhibit and that there would be a dolphin show right before lunchtime. (5) Dolphins are my favorite animal, so I knew that I had to see that show!

(6) Once we made it inside the zoo, I found my group, which included my friends, Jordan and Caleb. (7) I told them how much I wanted to see the dolphin show, and they agreed to keep an eye on the time so we could all go see it. (8) We decided to see the Africa section of the zoo first, where we saw lions, zebras, gorillas, and a rhino. (9) Right after we saw the rhino, I looked at my watch and saw that we had 10 minutes until it started.

(10) "Oh, hey guys, it's time to go," I said and started walking away.

(11) Jordan and Caleb followed until Caleb said, "Guys, wait just a minute! (12) We missed the giraffes!" (13) Caleb darted over to the giraffes and began taking pictures of one standing right at the fence. (14) As he laughed and turned to look at us, the giraffe leaned its head down to him. (15) Before Caleb could react, the giraffe bit the strap of Caleb's camera and carried it away! (16) "No!" Caleb shouted.

(17) "We have to help him get it back!" Jordan exclaimed.

(18) I hesitated and looked at my watch, then sighed and said, "Yeah, but we need help."

(19) Jordan and I searched and searched, but we could not find any zoo employees nearby. (20) My watch beeped to let me know that it was noon, five minutes before the dolphin show started. (21) I had given up on seeing the show but knew that we still needed to find help before the giraffe destroyed the camera.

(22) A woman in a button-up shirt with the zoo's logo came hurrying down the walkway. (23) Jordan and I stopped her to tell her what had happened (24) We pointed to Caleb, who was still staring at the giraffe in dismay. (25) She laughed and said, "Well, lucky for you three, I know something about this giraffe here." (26) She took a small mirror from her pocket, tilted it toward the giraffe, and added, "He loves shiny things." (27) To our surprise, the giraffe walked back over to the fence and leaned its head toward the mirror. (28) "Get ready," the woman warned, and Caleb, Jordan, and I hurried to stand beneath the giraffe's head. (29) It finally dropped the camera, and Caleb dove and caught it.

(30) "Thank you!" Caleb said to her.

(31) "Oh, don't worry about it. (32) But I am running late for the dolphin show, and it can't start without me, so I need to go. (33) Enjoy the rest of your visit!"

(34) Jordan, Caleb, and I looked at each other and then bolted for the dolphin exhibit. (35) Just after the trainer we got there who had helped us. (36) We had a great time watching the dolphins follow her signals. (37) We continued talking about it as we went to meet the rest of our class for lunch. (38) That is, until Caleb announced, "Guys, I think I left my camera at the dolphin exhibit!"

29. There is an unnecessary sentence in the first paragraph. Which sentence should be removed from this paragraph?

a. Sentence 1
b. Sentence 2
c. Sentence 4
d. Sentence 5

30. The wording in sentence 9 is unclear. Which of the following phrases should be used to replace *it* in sentence 9?

a. the rhino
b. lunchtime
c. the dolphin show
d. the giraffe exhibit

31. A transition word is needed at the beginning of sentence 22. In the box below, write a transition word that would be effective at the beginning of sentence 22.

32. Which of the following sentences is the clearest revision of sentence 35?

a. We got there just after the trainer who had helped us.
b. Who had helped us just after we got there the trainer.
c. The trainer who had helped us just after we got there.
d. Just after the trainer who had helped us, we got there.

Chelsea wrote the following paper about her favorite book and movie series. Read the following paper and note the revisions that Chelsea should make. Once you have read her paper, answer the questions that follow it.

From the Pages to the Screen

(1) J.K. Rowling became one of the most popular writers in the world when she created a wizard named Harry Potter. (2) The seven novels in her series sold millions of copies. (3) Both the *Harry Potter* books and movies have brought in billion-dollar profits.

(4) *Harry Potter and the Philosopher's Stone* had been in print for a little over a year when Warner Bros. bought the rights to make it into a movie. (5) J.K. Rowling had great control over the movie. (6) Her book was set in England. (7) She made sure the movie was filmed and set in England as well. (8) She also insisted that all of the actors were British, and young Daniel Radcliffe was chosen to play Harry. (9) Since many of the actors were children, they looked different in each movie because they were still growing up. (10) Rowling worked closely with the actors, telling them things about their characters that *Harry Potter* readers didn't even know yet.

(11) J.K. Rowling's work helped make the movie a big success when it came out in 2001. (12) Although its title was changed to *Harry Potter and the Sorcerer's Stone*, the story was still true to the one she created in her first *Harry Potter* book. (13) Audiences loved the movie just as much as readers loved the book. (14) Rowling continued the book series, and each new *Harry Potter* book received its own movie version. (15) The movies also helped new readers discover the series, and the popularity of *Harry Potter* only grew with the release of the films.

(16) The popularity of the books and movies motivated J.K. Rowling to continue writing about the world and wizards she had created. (17) However, she decided to try writing about these things in a new way. (18) Instead of writing more novels, J.K. Rowling turned to writing for the screen. (19) This film was inspired by a textbook mentioned in the first *Harry Potter* book, which Rowling also released as a real book in 2001. (20) The first *Fantastic Beasts* film was also successful and began a new series of films that serve as prequels to the *Harry Potter* book series.

(21) The first *Harry Potter* movie came out in between the release of the fourth and fifth books in the series. (22) The books were published over a span of 10 years, and the movies were also released over a period of 10 years. (23) While there are seven books in the book series, there are eight movies in the film series. (24) This is because the final movie, *Harry Potter and the Deathly Hallows*, was released in two parts in 2010 and 2011. (25) With that, the original *Harry Potter* series came to an end.

33. Which of the following sentences would state the controlling idea more effectively than sentence 3?

a. She wrote seven novels for the book series, but there ended up being eight movies in the film series.
b. The books inspired not only a series of movies but also an extravagant theme park.
c. J.K. Rowling had not considered writing scripts for movies when she began writing the *Harry Potter* series.
d. This success gave her the chance to bring Harry Potter from the pages of her books to movie screens.

34. Using the lines below, write a complete sentence that combines sentences 6 and 7.

____

____

____

35. One of the sentences in paragraph 2 is unnecessary. Which sentence should be removed from paragraph 2?

a. Sentence 4
b. Sentence 5
c. Sentence 8
d. Sentence 9

36. Which of the following sentences is a supporting detail that should be added after sentence 18?

a. In 2016, a movie called *Fantastic Beasts and Where to Find Them* was released in theaters.
b. A play about the *Harry Potter* characters was also written, but Rowling did not write it.
c. Rowling wanted to write about new characters, not just Harry Potter and his friends.
d. Since Rowling had had so much success with *Harry Potter*, she was inspired to write more.

37. Which sentence should be added after sentence 25 to improve the conclusion of the passage?

a. The *Fantastic Beasts* movies are considered to be their own series.
b. Fans can still experience the stories by reading the books over again.
c. But that wonderful wizard continues to be just as popular as ever.
d. J.K. Rowling can now put down the pen and enjoy her success.

Editing

Theresa is writing a narrative about a dancer named Samantha. Read the following paragraphs from the body of her story and look for errors that she needs to correct. Once you have read the paragraph, answer the questions that follow.

Taking Tap

(1) Last year, when Samantha signed up to take dance classes, she had to choose to learn either tap nor ballet. (2) She chose tap, and as she walked into class over a year later, she was still excited to learn more. (3) Samantha slipped into her tap shoes and began to warm up on the wooden floor. (4) Tap shoes are like dress shoes with little metal plates under the toes and the heels. (5) The plates are attached by small screws which can be loosened to change the sound of the tapping. (6) Ms. Jessica, one of Samantha's dance instructors, started the music. (7) Samantha and her friends started working on they're tap steps while watching themselves in the mirrors on the wall. (8) Samantha started with basic tap steps, called single steps, and quickly moved through different steps like the brush, the shuffle, and the ball change. (9) Samantha loves the modern movements and music of tap.

38. Which change would correct the mistake in sentence 1?

a. Remove the comma after *year.*
b. Change *dance classes* to *Dance Classes.*
c. Change *learn* to *learning.*
d. Change *nor* to *or.*

39. Which change would correct the mistake in sentence 4?

a. Change *are* to *is.*
b. Change *metal* to *metel.*
c. Add a comma after *plates.*
d. No change is needed in sentence 4.

40. Which change would correct the mistake in sentence 5?

a. Change *are* to *were.*
b. Change *which* to *that.*
c. Add a comma after *sound.*
d. Change *tapping* to *taping.*

41. Which change would correct the mistake in sentence 7?

a. Change *her* to *she.*
b. Change *they're* to *their.*
c. Change *themselves* to *theirselves.*
d. Change *on* to *from.*

Kenneth is writing an essay about metamorphosis. Read the first two paragraphs from the body of Kenneth's essay and look for errors that he needs to correct. Once you have read the paragraphs, answer the questions that follow them.

Amazing Metamorphosis

(1) When butterflies are the most well-known insects that undergo complete metamorphosis, there are several other insects that also go through this amazing process. (2) Some of these insects include beetles, flies, ants, bees, wasps, and fleas.

(3) Some insects go through what is called incomplete metamorphosis. (4) Incomplete metamorphosis is different from complete metamorphosis. (5) In incomplete metamorphosis, insects does not go through the pupal stage of complete metamorphosis. (6) The three phases of incomplete metamorphosis include the egg (the first stage), nymph (the second stage), and adult (the last stage) stages. (7) In the nymph stage, instead of the insect becoming a caterpillar, the nymph is a smaller version of the adult insect, and it does not have wings. (8) The insect then becomes an adult by shedding it's outer skeleton and developing wings. (9) Some of the insects that undergo incomplete metamorphosis included crickets, grasshoppers, cockroaches and stinkbugs.

42. Which change would correct the mistake in sentence 1?

a. Change *When* to *Even Though.*
b. Change *butterflies are* to *butterflies were.*
c. Remove the comma after *metamorphosis.*
d. Change *there* to *they.*

43. Which change would correct the mistake in sentence 5?

a. Remove the comma after *metamorphosis*
b. Change *does* to *do.*
c. Change *of* to *for.*
d. No change is needed in sentence 5.

44. Which change would correct the mistake in sentence 8?

a. Add a comma after *then.*
b. Change *becomes* to *become.*
c. Change *it's* to *its.*
d. Change *developing* to *developed.*

45. Select the correct verb to use in sentence 9.

Some of the insects that undergo incomplete metamorphosis ____________ crickets, grasshoppers, cockroaches, and stinkbugs.

included
will include
have included
include

Answer Key and Explanations for Test #1

Reading

1. C: TEKS Standard (6.2)(B)

Fog can make it difficult to see things that are far away, and it can make nearby objects look different than they normally do. This means that, in line 8, the word *distorts* is most like the word *changes*. Choice C is correct. Because distorts is used to describe an effect on a person's vision, not hearing, choice A is incorrect. The fog's effects do not improve, or sharpen, a person's vision, so choice B is incorrect. The fog changes the way things look but does not stop a person from seeing everything, so choice D is incorrect.

2. C: TEKS Standard (6.9)(D)

The poet uses a metaphor in line 2 by calling fog a 'dense, gray blanket.' The poet says this because fog often looks like a thick layer, or like a covering over an area. It is also usually thick enough to make things hard to see. These characteristics of fog are similar to a dense blanket, so choice C is correct. While the poem describes the fog as eerie and haunting in lines 5 and 10, the metaphor in line 2 does not compare the fog to a ghost, so choice A is incorrect. The fog does have dialogue later in the poem. However, comparing the fog to a blanket does not describe the noises it can make, so choice B is incorrect. Line 2 does not describe the fog's movement, so choice D is incorrect.

3. D: TEKS Standard (6.5)(F)

The poem says that fog "fades as quickly as it came," which shows that the effects it has are not permanent. This means that choice D is correct. Although the poem says that fog "smothers landscapes," the poem does not suggest that fog is deadly. Additionally, the rest of the poem describes fog as sneaky, not dangerous, so choice A is incorrect. Since fog "smothers landscapes," it does not only occur near water, so choice B is incorrect. The poem does not explain how often fog appears, so choice C is incorrect.

4. A: TEKS Standard (6.7)(A)

The fog is described using multiple words that are associated with mystery, such as *eerie, haunting*, and *creeps*. The poem has a mysterious theme, and the fog is portrayed as a traveler, so choice A is correct. Though the poem says that fog "seeps in from the sea," the poem does not include details that suggest it takes place on an island, so choice B is incorrect. Choice C is incorrect because the poem describes fog, not any other type of cloudy weather. Choice D is incorrect because the poem only describes the qualities of fog. It does not give a scientific explanation of fog.

5. B: TEKS Standard (6.8)(B)

In the last line, the poet describes how quickly fog goes away. By using only two lines at the end of the poem, instead of four, the poet leads the reader to read the last stanza quickly. This illustrates how rapidly fog disappears, so choice B is correct. The poem does not suggest that fog is boring. Additionally, a poet would most likely use long lines or stanzas to show this, so choice A is incorrect. The fog is described as thick, not thin, so choice C is incorrect. The fog's desires are not described in the poem. Since the words in the poem do not support this idea, choice D is incorrect.

6. D: TEKS Standard (6.6)(C)

Something that "distorts the vision" would make it difficult to see things, so choice D is correct. The line "clutching rooftops, climbing trees" describes how fog appears to move, not how it affects a person's vision. This makes choice A incorrect. The line "it fills the mind and fools the feet" shows that fog can confuse people or cause them to get lost. While this may be caused by the fog's effect on a person's vision, it does not directly describe an impact on vision. Choice B is incorrect. The line "its eerie whisper fills the land" describes what sounds might come with fog but not how fog impacts vision, so choice C is incorrect.

7. A: TEKS Standard (6.9)(F)

Fog is not something that can be caught. The fog teases the readers by telling them to catch it, even though they cannot. This shows that the fog is fleeting, or temporary. Additionally, the poet says that the fog does this using an "eerie whisper." *Eerie* is similar to *mysterious* or *creepy*, so the fog's eerie whisper and its words create a tone of mystery. Choice A is correct. Choice B is incorrect because these lines do not show that fog looks or behaves in a dark way. The poem also does not have a sad tone. The fog's speech in these lines is not friendly since it taunts the readers. Also, the overall tone of the poem is not hopeful, so choice C is incorrect. Fog gives the reader an impossible task, but not a dangerous one. Additionally, the poem does not have a cautionary tone, so choice D is incorrect.

8. D: TEKS Standard (6.5)(C)

Paragraph 3 lists the items that Tommy and his dad packed to put in the geocaches. Paragraph 9 explains that Sam got to choose an item to trade since he found the first geocache. These events show that items are traded as part of each geocache hunt. Choice D is correct because it is reasonable to predict that another item will be traded when they find another geocache. There is no reason to predict that the boys will find an equal number of geocaches, so choice A is incorrect. In paragraph 5, Mr. Jones explains that coordinates for each geocache are input into a GPS. This is a necessary step for finding a geocache, so choice B is incorrect. The passage does not include information that suggests that Sam would be upset if someone else found the geocache. Additionally, paragraph 2 says Sam always has fun with Tommy and his dad. These facts show that choice C is incorrect.

9. B: TEKS Standard (6.7)(C)

Sam finding the cache is the highest point of the plot, or the climax. The events that lead up to this event, the rising action, build suspense and create conflict as Sam experiences geocaching for the first time. The result of the conflict occurs when Sam finds the cache, so choice B is correct. Tommy and his dad picking up Sam is part of the rising action, so choice A is incorrect. The GPS coordinates are part of the rising action, so they are not the climax of the story, and choice C is incorrect. Choice D is incorrect because the group sets off to find the next cache after the climax of the story has occurred.

10. TEKS Standard (6.5)(H)

Part A: D: In paragraphs 7 and 8, the GPS only takes Tommy, Mr. Jones, and Sam to the area the cache is in. It does not take them to the exact location. This shows that GPS coordinates may take geocachers near a cache, but not to its exact location, so choice D is correct. The reader cannot conclude that only one cache was hidden in the park where the group searched. At the beginning of the story, Mr. Jones explained to Tommy that he had found a couple of new geocaches to hunt for, so choice A is incorrect. The cache is described as "medium sized." This shows that other caches may be smaller or larger, so choice B is incorrect. Although the cache in the story was found in a park, these paragraphs do not support the idea that parks are the most common locations for geocaches, so choice C is incorrect.

Part B: A: Choice A is correct because it shows that the GPS is not completely accurate and that geocachers may have to look around for the cache. Choice B is incorrect because it simply describes the first place that the GPS led them to. In this sentence, the GPS is still leading them to the cache. So, this sentence does not show how close the GPS led them to the cache. Choice C is incorrect because it describes the size of the cache. This sentence does not give the reader any information about the accuracy of the GPS. Choice D is incorrect because it describes the trio's actions. It does not show the reader how close the GPS will get them to the cache.

11. B: TEKS Standard (6.6)(D)

The summary in choice B most accurately describes the story's events in the order that they happened, so it is correct. Choice A is incorrect because the passage shows that Sam wanted to go geocaching, even though he did not know what it was. Choice C is incorrect because it only includes minor details and does not accurately describe the main conflict of the story. Choice D is incorrect because it suggests that the trio was not looking for a geocache and only found it by accident.

12. A: TEKS Standard (6.7)(B)

Sam does not fully understand geocaching at first, and he is confused by the activity. When he finds the cache, he understands why the activity is fun and becomes excited, so choice A is correct. This event is the resolution of the story's conflict. While Mr. Jones and Tommy helped Sam understand how to find the cache, the story is not about Sam's reliance on others, so choice B is incorrect. Sam selecting an item for the cache is a minor detail in the story and does not affect the plot, so choice C is incorrect. The passage does not tell the reader why Sam has never been geocaching before, so choice D is incorrect.

13. C: TEKS Standard (6.5)(F)

Mr. Jones says that geocaching is "a giant worldwide treasure hunt" where containers are hidden for other people to find. Since Tommy, Mr. Jones, and Sam have found the container and left a prize in it, they want others to also be able to find it, so choice C is correct. The passage does not show that their packs are too full to take the geocache container with them. Additionally, geocaching does not involve taking the entire container, so choice A is incorrect. The passage also does not say that they did not like the treasure in the cache, so choice B is incorrect. Hiding the treasure back where it was found will not confuse others. It will allow other geocachers to use the same GPS coordinates to locate the cache, so choice D is incorrect.

14. B: TEKS Standard (6.2)(C)

Since *geo-* means *earth*, then the meaning of the word *geocache* must have something to do with the ground or the outdoors. In the story, Mr. Jones explains that geocaching takes place all over the world. Sam, Tommy, and Mr. Jones are looking for a geocache that is hidden outdoors. When they find it, it is a container with objects inside. Choice B describes the object that the trio in the story found. It also is related to the prefix *geo-* since it specifies that the object is outdoors, so choice B is correct. The material that the container is made of is not mentioned in the passage. The prefix *geo-* would only refer to materials that come from the ground, not all natural materials. For these reasons, choice A is incorrect. The object in the story was not buried underground, so choice C is incorrect. The trio was trying to find the location of the object. They did not use it to figure out where they were on Earth, so choice D is incorrect.

15. C: TEKS Standard (6.8)(A)

Realistic fiction includes events that could actually occur. Since the events and people in "Geocaching" are not out of the ordinary and could happen in real life, choice C is correct. This story does not imagine a historical event, so choice A is incorrect. A fictional story that involves an unexplained event is a mystery. "Geocaching" is not a mystery, since there are explanations for the events in the story, so choice B is incorrect. No crime occurs in the passage, so choice D is incorrect.

16. C: TEKS Standard (6.9)(E)

A third-person omniscient point of view allows the author to include each character's unspoken thoughts and feelings. For example, in paragraph 2, the author tells the reader that Sam does not understand what geocaching is. Additionally, in paragraph 6, the author tells the reader that Mr. Jones knows Sam is confused and thinks he will catch on, so choice C is correct. The process and gear needed for geocaching could be shown without a third-person omniscient point of view, so choice A is incorrect. Sam's excitement about the cache is shown through Sam's dialogue, so choice B is incorrect. Mr. Jones explains the value of GPS coordinates out loud, so this information would be known if the author had used a first-person point of view. This makes choice D incorrect.

17. B, E: TEKS Standard (6.5)(F)

The story describes the job of each Morgan family member on the ranch, and it mentions that the working dogs, such as Shep, also have jobs. Additionally, the passage says that Marcus's family owns the ranch. This information supports the conclusions in choices B and E, so they are correct. Beef and dairy cattle are raised on the ranch, but the passage does not say that people visit the ranch to buy them, so choice A is incorrect. The story also does not tell the reader the number of cattle or sheep at the ranch, only that the sheep herd is small, which makes choice C incorrect. While some of the animals are used for food, such as the cows and chickens, the passage does not suggest that the working dogs and sheep are used for food, so choice D is incorrect.

18. D: TEKS Standard (6.6)(C)

The sentence in choice D states that the sheep get their wool sheared every spring. This shows that the role of the sheep is to produce wool, so choice D is correct. Choice A says that sheep live on the ranch, but it is incorrect because it does not show the purpose of the sheep. Choices B and C explain how Marcus takes care of the sheep, but they do not explain the purpose that the sheep on the ranch serve. Choices B and C are incorrect.

19. B: TEKS Standard (6.9)(A)

The author provides details about living on a ranch that show the reader that it is hard work, so choice B is correct. These details include the daily jobs each family member has and the early time at which they wake up to start their chores. While the story tells the reader about Marcus' brothers, James and Robert, it does not describe their relationship, so choice A is incorrect. The passage describes the use and importance of other animals, like the sheep and the working dogs. The passage does not argue that cows are the most useful animals on the ranch, so choice C is incorrect. The working dogs' jobs are described in the passage, but the passage is not about the working dogs, so choice D is incorrect.

20. C: TEKS Standard (6.5)(G)

Paragraph 3 explains that the Assateague ponies do not have regular contact with rangers and that they live as wild animals. Choice C is correct. The passage does not suggest that the Assateague ponies are endangered, so choice A is incorrect. The size of the Assateague ponies is described in paragraph 2, not paragraph 3, which makes choice B incorrect. Paragraph 3 says the Assateague ponies are "left alone to survive," but it does not compare the treatment of the Assateague and Chincoteague ponies. This makes choice D incorrect.

21. A: TEKS Standard (6.9)(B)

The passage begins with general information about the ponies' island habitat and their similar appearances. It then gives specific information describing how the two herds of ponies are treated by humans. This structure shows the reader that even though the ponies are very similar, they are treated differently, so choice A is correct. Choice B is incorrect because the passage does not describe the experience of being near the ponies. The story gives facts about the ponies and is not meant to entertain the reader, so choice C is incorrect. While the Chincoteague pony sale is described in the passage, the author gives information about the Assateague ponies, too, so choice D is incorrect.

22. A: TEKS Standard (6.5)(H)

Paragraphs 4 through 6 explain that the Chincoteague ponies can be bought at a special sale, which many people attend each year to see the ponies. This supports choice A, so it is correct. While some details about the sale are described in these paragraphs, the price of the ponies is not described, so choice B is incorrect. While these paragraphs do say that veterinarians check on the ponies and try to keep them healthy, they do not suggest that the ponies never become ill. This makes choice C incorrect. Choice D is incorrect because these paragraphs state that the Chincoteague ponies are used to being around humans because of the visits from veterinarians.

23. B: TEKS Standard (6.8)(Di)

The passage shows that, even though the ponies live on the same island and look alike, the Assateague ponies are left alone and the Chincoteague ponies are treated by veterinarians. This is summarized in choice B, so it is the correct answer. While Assateague Island is where both types of ponies live, the island itself is not the main topic of the passage, so choice A is incorrect. The fact that the Chincoteague ponies receive checkups from a veterinarian shows how they are cared for, but it is not the main idea of the passage, so choice C is incorrect. The passage is about both groups of horses, not just the Assateague horses, so choice D is incorrect.

24. C: TEKS Standard (6.8)(Diii)

The author describes the similarities between the two herds and the differences in how they are treated. This is done using a compare-and-contrast structure, so choice C is correct. The author describes how the Chincoteague ponies are cared for but does not include a step-by-step process, so choice A incorrect. The passage says that humans have left the Assateague ponies alone. However, the passage does not say that this has caused the Assateague ponies to dislike humans, so choice B is incorrect. Choice D is incorrect because the passage discusses buying a pony but does not describe the advantages and disadvantages of having one.

25. C: TEKS Standard (6.5)(E)

In "Life on a Ranch," each animal has a purpose. For example, the sheep provide wool, the cows provide beef and dairy, and the working dogs herd sheep. In "Island Ponies," neither type of pony has a specific purpose on the island, so choice C is correct. Choice A is incorrect because "Life on a Ranch" does not explain whether or not the animals are sold for money. Additionally, in "Island Ponies," the Assateague ponies are not sold for money, only the Chincoteague ponies are. The reader can infer that the animals in "Life on a Ranch" all spend time with humans because the animals belong to the Morgan family and are cared for by the family. The Chincoteague ponies are similar, as many people come to the pony sale to look at and buy them, so choice B is incorrect. Choice D is incorrect because not all of the animals in "Life on a Ranch" are used for food, such as the working dogs.

26. D: TEKS Standard (6.5)(E)

In "Life on a Ranch," Marcus checks the sheep for injuries as part of his chores every evening. In "Island Ponies," the Chincoteague ponies get checkups from a veterinarian twice a year, so choice D is correct. While the Chincoteague ponies receive care, they do not receive care every day, so choice A is incorrect. Choice B is incorrect since neither passage mentions the type of food that is given to the sheep nor the Chincoteague ponies. Choice C is incorrect because only the Assateague ponies are usually left alone, not the Chincoteague ponies or the sheep.

27. C: TEKS Standard (6.5)(E)

Paragraph 5 of "Life on a Ranch" says that the sheep are sheared for their wool every spring. Paragraph 5 of "Island Ponies" states that the ponies are available at a yearly sale every July. This means that choice C is correct. Paragraph 5 of "Island Ponies" does not describe what it is like to own one of the Chincoteague ponies, so choice A is incorrect. Neither passage provides any information about how the animals in the passage find food, so choice B is incorrect. Paragraph 5 of both passages tells the reader about some interaction of the animals with humans. However, paragraph 5 of "Life on a Ranch" does not say that the sheep enjoy being around humans, so choice D is incorrect.

Extended Response

27. TEKS Standard (6.11)(C)

Please use the rubric below to make sure your response meets these criteria. Try to have a friend or family member grade your response for you or take a break after writing your response and return to grade it yourself with fresh eyes.

Below is an excerpt of the STAAR Grades 6-EII Argumentative/Opinion Writing Rubric.

<table>
<tr><th>Score Point</th><th>Development and Organization of Ideas</th></tr>
<tr><td>3</td><td><ul>
<li>Argument/opinion is clear and fully developed
The argument/opinion is clearly identifiable. The focus is consistent throughout, creating a response that is unified and easy to follow.</li>
<li>Organization is effective
A purposeful structure that includes an effective introduction and conclusion is evident. The organizational structure is appropriate and effectively supports the development of the argument/opinion. The sentences, paragraphs, or ideas are logically connected in purposeful and highly effective ways.</li>
<li>Evidence is specific, well chosen, and relevant
The response includes relevant text-based evidence that is clearly explained and consistently supports and develops the argument/opinion. For pairs in grades 6 through EII, evidence is drawn from both texts. The response reflects a thorough understanding of the writing purpose.</li>
<li>Expression of ideas is clear and effective
The writer's word choice is specific, purposeful, and enhances the response. Almost all sentences and phrases are effectively crafted to convey the writer's ideas and contribute to the overall quality of the response and the clarity of the message.</li>
</ul></td></tr>
<tr><th>Score Point</th><th>Conventions</th></tr>
<tr><td>2</td><td>Student writing demonstrates consistent command of grade-level-appropriate conventions, including correct:<ul>
<li>sentence construction</li>
<li>punctuation</li>
<li>capitalization</li>
<li>grammar</li>
<li>spelling</li>
</ul>The response has few errors, but those errors do not impact the clarity of the writing.</td></tr>
</table>

Revising

29. B: TEKS Standard (6.10)(Bii)

Choice B is correct because sentence 2 gives the reader unnecessary information. The items in the speaker's backpack do not help the reader understand the information in the rest of the paragraph. Choice A is incorrect because sentence 1 shows the reader the setting of the story. It also describes how the narrator is feeling, which helps the reader understand the story better. Choice C is incorrect because sentence 4 gives the reader information that impacts the story's plot. Choice D is incorrect because sentence 5 supports the information in sentence 4. It also helps the reader understand the speaker's later actions in sentence 18.

30. C: TEKS Standard (6.10)(C)

Sentence 9 says that there are 10 minutes until something starts. Sentence 4 shows that the dolphin show begins at a certain time. Sentence 7 states that the boys want to keep an eye on the time so they can attend the dolphin show. This shows that choice C is correct since the narrator is making sure they leave on time to go to the dolphin show. Choice A is incorrect because the rhino is an animal, not an event or process. It would not make sense to say that the rhino will start in 10 minutes. Sentence 4 says that the dolphin show happens before lunch. Sentence 8 says that the boys went to the Africa exhibit first. Since they are leaving the exhibit and have not been to the dolphin show yet, choice B is incorrect. Choice D is incorrect because the giraffe exhibit is a location, not an event like a show. The giraffe exhibit is always there, so it does not start at a certain time.

31. TEKS Standard (6.10)(Bi)

Sentence 22 says that a woman who works at the zoo hurried toward the boys. In sentence 19, Jordan and the narrator are struggling to find a zoo employee to help them. Sentence 20 shows that they have been looking for a few minutes. The transition at the beginning of sentence 22 should show that the boys have been looking for a while before the woman arrives. *Finally* and *eventually* are both examples of transition words that would be effective at the beginning of sentence 22.

32. A: TEKS Standard (6.10)(C)

Sentence 35 should tell the reader that the boys arrived at the dolphin show right after the trainer arrived. Choice A is clear and tells the reader this information, so it is correct. Choice B is incorrect because it is not clear or grammatically correct. Choice C is incorrect because it forms an incomplete sentence. Choice D is incorrect because it does not tell the reader the information in a way that is clear and easy to read. Choice A is clearer than choice D.

33. D: TEKS Standard (6.10)(Bi)

This passage is about how J.K. Rowling's *Harry Potter* series was so successful that it was turned into a series of movies. The controlling idea should clearly state this idea to tell the reader what the passage is about. This idea is most clearly stated in choice D, so it is correct. Choice A simply tells the reader how many books are in the book series and how many movies are in the film series. This does not help the reader understand what the passage is about, so choice A is incorrect. The passage is about movies that came from the *Harry Potter* franchise. It is not about the theme park, so choice B is incorrect. Choice C tells the reader a detail that is related to movies and the *Harry Potter* series. However, it is incorrect because it does not help the reader understand the purpose of the passage.

34. TEKS Standard (6.10)(C)

Sentence 6 says that *Harry Potter and the Philosopher's Stone* is set in England. Sentence 7 says that J.K. Rowling made sure that the movie was also filmed and set in England. The information in sentence 6 caused the information in sentence 7. The new sentence should include this information and show the relationship between these facts. The new sentence should be similar to the following sentence: Her book was set in England, so she made sure that the movie was filmed and set in England as well. The sentence should also be grammatically correct, complete, and clear.

35. D: TEKS Standard (6.10)(Bii)

Sentence 9 does not help the reader understand the rest of the information in the paragraph. It does not support the information in sentences 8 or 9. Sentence 9 is also not relevant to the passage, so choice D is correct. Choice A is incorrect because sentence 4 tells the reader about an event that is important to the passage. This event led to all of the other events described, so this sentence is needed. Choice B is incorrect because sentence 5 contains information that helps the reader understand sentences 7, 8, and 10. Choice C is incorrect because sentence 8 is a supporting detail for sentence 5.

36. A: TEKS Standard (6.10)(Bii)

Sentence 18 says that J.K. Rowling decided to write something that would become a movie instead of a book. Sentence 19 describes a movie that was based on another book that J.K. Rowling wrote. The sentence added after sentence 19 should show a connection between these sentences. Choice A is correct because it says when the movie that Rowling wrote came out. This supports sentence 18, and it helps the reader understand the information in sentence 19. Choice B is unrelated to sentence 18 since it describes a play that was not written by Rowling, so it is incorrect. Choice C is incorrect because it does not support sentence 18. It also does not help the reader understand sentence 19. Choice D is incorrect because it restates the information given in sentence 16. Choice D does not give the reader new information or support sentence 18.

37. C: TEKS Standard (6.10)(Bi)

The last sentence in the conclusion should be related to the overall topic of the passage. It should also not focus on a supporting detail or tell the reader new details. The topic of the passage is the popularity of the Harry Potter books and movies. Choice C is related to this topic. It also summarizes the idea of the passage by saying that Harry Potter and Rowling's works are still very popular, so choice C is correct. Choice A is incorrect because it focuses on a supporting detail, not the overall purpose of the passage. Choice B is incorrect because it is not related to the topic or purpose of the passage. Choice D is incorrect because it introduces a new idea by discussing what J.K. Rowling may do next.

Editing

38. D: TEKS Standard (6.10)(Dvi)

Neither and *nor* and *either* and *or* are both pairs of correlating conjunctions. This means that the conjunctions in each pair work together to create meaning in a sentence. *Neither* and *nor* must be used together, and *either* and *or* must be used together. Sentence 1 says that Samantha had to choose either tap nor ballet, but this does not make sense. Because the sentence uses *either*, it must also use *or*, not *nor*, so choice D is correct. "Last year" is a prepositional phrase used to start the sentence. It is acceptable for this phrase to end in a comma, so choice A is incorrect. Sentence 1 does not name a specific dance class, and *dance classes* is not a proper noun. There is no need to capitalize *dance classes*, so choice b is incorrect. *Learning* is used to show that someone is currently learning something. However, in sentence 1, Samantha had not started learning to dance, so choice C is incorrect.

39. D: TEKS Standard (6.10)(D)

Sentence 4 does not contain any errors in spelling or grammar, so choice D is correct. *Are* is a plural noun, and *is* is a singular noun. *Tap shoes* is a plural noun that should be used with a plural verb. *Are* is used correctly in sentence 4, so choice A is incorrect. *Metel* is a misspelling of *metal*, so choice B is incorrect. There is no reason to add a comma after the word *plates* in sentence 4, so choice C is incorrect.

40. B: TEKS Standard (6.10)(Dv)

Relative pronouns, such as *which* and *that*, are used to give more information about a noun or pronoun in a sentence. *Which* is used to show that the words that come after it are not needed for the sentence to make sense and give enough information. *That* is used to show that the information is needed for the sentence to make sense and give enough information. In sentence 5, the information about what the screws are used for is important and adds information. This information is needed in the sentence, so *that* should be used, and choice B is correct. Choice A is incorrect because *plates* is a plural noun that should be used with a plural verb, like *are*. There is no need to add a comma after *sound*, so choice C is incorrect. Since the word *tap* ends with one vowel and one consonant, the last consonant must be doubled when a suffix that begins with a vowel is added to it. *Tapping* includes a doubled *p*, so choice D is incorrect.

41. B: TEKS Standard (6.10)(Dix)

They're is a contraction for *they* and *are*. *Their* is a possessive pronoun. Since the dance students are doing the tap steps and the steps belong to them, *their* is the correct word to use. Choice B is correct. In sentence 7, *her* is used as a possessive pronoun to show that the friends belong to Samantha. *Her* is used correctly, so choice A is incorrect. *Theirselves* is not a word. It is a word commonly mistaken for *themselves*, so choice C is incorrect. A reflection is described as being in a mirror, not on a mirror. The dancers in sentence 7 were also not standing on top of the mirrors. *On* would not make sense in sentence 7, so choice D is incorrect.

42. A: TEKS Standard (6.10)(Dvi)

This sentence states that while butterflies are the most famous insects that go through complete metamorphosis, there are many others, as well. Currently, the sentence begins with *when*. This suggests that other insects only go through complete metamorphosis when butterflies are the most well-known. That is not accurate. Changing *when* to *even though* makes the sentence clearer and more accurate, so choice A is correct. *Are* is a present tense verb, and *were* is a past tense verb. Sentence 1 is in the present tense, so it needs to use present tense verbs like *are*. Choice B is incorrect. Sentence 1 is a complex sentence because it is made of a dependent clause and an independent clause. When a complex sentence begins with a dependent clause, the clause should end with a comma. The comma after *metamorphosis* is needed, so choice C is incorrect. If *there* were changed to *they*, the sentence would suggest that butterflies are several other insects. This is not logical, so choice D is incorrect.

43. B: TEKS Standard (6.10)(Div)

Does is a singular verb, and *do* is a plural verb. *Insects* is a plural noun, so it must be used with a plural verb, like *do*. This makes choice B correct. "In complete metamorphosis" is a prepositional phrase, and it appears at the beginning of the sentence. Usually, a prepositional phrase that begins a sentence ends with a comma, so choice A is incorrect. Changing *of* to *for* in sentence 5 would make the sentence less clear, so choice C is incorrect. Because there is an error in subject-verb agreement in sentence 5, choice D is incorrect.

44. C: TEKS Standard (6.10)(Dix)

It's is a contraction of *it* and *is*. *Its* is a possessive pronoun. Sentence 8 says that adult insects shed their outer skin, so the outer skin belongs to them. *Its* is the correct word to use in sentence 8 since it can stand in for *insects* to communicate the correct meaning. Choice C is correct. The word *then* is not used as an introductory word in this sentence, and there is no other reason to add a comma after it in sentence 8. Choice A is incorrect. In the present tense, *become* is a plural verb and *becomes* is a singular verb. *Insect* is a singular verb, so it should be used with the singular verb *becomes*. Choice B is incorrect. *Developing*, by itself, is a present tense verb. *Developed*, by itself, is a past tense verb. This sentence is in the present tense, so *developing* is used correctly, and choice D is incorrect.

45. include: TEKS Standard (6.10)(Dii)

Sentence 9, like the rest of the passage, is in the present tense. This means that sentence 9 must use present tense verbs. Of the provided choices, only *include* is a present tense verb. *Include* is in the correct tense and makes sense in the sentence, so it is the correct answer. *Included* and *have included* refer to events in the past, so neither of these verbs fit well in this sentence. *Will include* refers to events in the future, so it is also not correct for this sentence.

Practice Test #2

Reading

The Talent Show

(1) The first notes floated from the piano. Megan smiled, warm and excited beneath the glaring stage lights. This was her moment. She had practiced. She had prepared. She was ready. As the introduction ended, Megan opened her mouth and began to sing.

(2) The song flowed along, and Megan relaxed, scanning the faces of the audience. But somewhere in the middle of the second verse, her mind suddenly went blank. The music went on, but the words were gone. Megan's smile faded. She stood silently with her mouth hanging open. When the music finally trickled to a stop, Megan ran from the stage.

(3) In a cramped dressing room backstage, Megan buried her face in her hands. She had wanted so much to win this talent show. Tears seeped between her fingers. Her confidence, pride, and excitement had been replaced by utter disappointment. She felt a hand on her shoulder and lifted her damp face.

(4) "Ella and Kaylee are here," Megan's mom said, giving her shoulder a quick squeeze.

(5) Ella and Kaylee, Megan's two best friends, pulled folding chairs over to face Megan. She looked at them forlornly.

(6) "I'm a total failure," she moaned.

(7) Ella and Kaylee exchanged glances. Kaylee reached out and squeezed Megan's hand.

(8) "What are you talking about?" Kaylee said. "That first verse was some of your best singing ever."

(9) "Thanks," Megan said. "But the problem is that the first verse is all I sang. Then I totally bombed. I can't believe I forgot the words after all that practice."

(10) "You didn't totally bomb," Ella said. "You just forgot the words. That happens to everybody. Besides, don't the pros say you should leave your audience wanting more?"

(11) "I guess so," Megan admitted.

(12) "Well, trust me," Ella said. "I guarantee they wanted more—like the rest of the song! You probably did, too."

(13) Megan smiled a little. "So, you guys don't think I'm a total dork for forgetting the words?"

(14) "Of course not," Kaylee said. "Forgetting the words doesn't make you a dork. It just makes you human. And you're still the most talented person I know."

(15) Ella nodded in agreement. Megan pulled Ella and Kaylee into a quick hug. Then she wiped her eyes and managed to give a genuine smile.

(16) "I'm so lucky to have best friends like you two," Megan said. "It's nice to know that you'll be my friends forever, no matter what!"

The Tournament

(1) Looking for a hole in the defense, Scott dribbled the ball, shifting it from hand to hand. A trickle of sweat ran down his back. No one was open. There were only seconds left on the clock, and Scott knew he had a difficult decision to make.

(2) The other team was leading by two points, and Scott was just outside the three-point line. If he could make the shot, the Eagles would be state champions again. But if he missed ... Scott didn't want to think about that. He knew what he had to do.

(3) It was a classic jump shot. The ball left his hands and sailed toward the basket in a perfect arc. The crowd, the other players, and the whole stadium seemed frozen in time. All eyes were on the ball as it struck the rim and bounced off. The buzzer blared. The game was over. Scott had missed, and the Eagles had lost.

(4) Scott became a statue on the court as people surged around him. Elated family members swarmed the winning team. Teammates hugged and slapped each other on the back. Even Scott's teammates joined in the celebration.

(5) Suddenly, Scott felt himself being hoisted unsteadily onto the shoulders of his friends. Over the loudspeaker, the announcer proclaimed that Scott had been named the most valuable player of the championship game. Everyone cheered, and the Eagles took a victory lap with Scott on their shoulders. Finally, Scott's friends put him back on solid ground.

(6) Scott was bewildered. He was the one who missed the most important shot of the game. How could anyone call him the most valuable player? He didn't feel very valuable at the moment. Scott approached Coach Travis.

(7) "Coach," Scott said, "there must be some mistake. I can't be the most valuable player."

(8) "There's no mistake," Coach Travis said. "You had 26 points, 11 rebounds, and 8 assists. I'd say that makes you a very valuable player."

(9) "But I missed that last shot," Scott said. "We lost the game because of me."

(10) "I don't know about that," said Coach Travis. "Everybody misses a shot from time to time. Don't be so hard on yourself. It's all about perspective."

(11) "What do you mean?" Scott asked.

(12) "Well," Coach Travis answered, "you could say you are the reason we lost the game because you missed that last shot. On the other hand, you could say you are the reason we almost won because of your awesome performance throughout the game. How you look at it is up to you."

(13) Scott's teammates came running over and surrounded Coach Travis. They jostled one another playfully, talking and laughing.

(14) "Hey, Coach," one player called out, "how about treating your team to pizza?"

(15) "I don't know," said Coach Travis. "Do you think you deserve pizza?"

(16) Scott piped up. "Of course we do! After all, we almost won the game."

(17) Coach Travis smiled. "You're right, Scott. We did almost win. Okay, pizza for everyone!"

Refer to the passage "The Talent Show" to answer questions 1-4.

1. What is the main theme of this story?

a. Real friends support you, no matter what.
b. It is easy to forget the words of a song.
c. Performing in a talent show can be embarrassing.
d. Megan feels like a failure.

2. Why does Kaylee say what she says in paragraph 8?

a. To cheer Megan up by making a joke about her performance
b. To make Megan feel better about what she did sing
c. To distract Megan from the fact that she did not finish the song
d. To help Megan forget that she did not finish the song

3. Which of the following facts about the story shows that it is realistic fiction?

a. The story's setting is not described using many details.
b. All of the story's main characters have dialogue.
c. The story has a beginning, a middle, and an end.
d. The events in the story are possible and likely to happen.

4. How do the events in paragraph 2 contribute to the conflict of the story?

a. They show why Megan thought she would win the talent show.
b. They show why Megan became upset and hid backstage.
c. They show why Megan was avoiding Ella and Kaylee.
d. They show why Megan forgot the words to the song she was singing.

Refer to the passage "The Tournament" to answer questions 5-8.

5. Why does the author use a metaphor to describe Scott's actions in the first sentence of paragraph 4?

a. To show how alarming the crowd was to Scott
b. To show how proud Scott was of his performance
c. To show how focused Scott was at the end of the game
d. To show how dismayed Scott was that they had lost

6. Which of the following is the best summary of this story?

a. At the buzzer, Scott misses an important basket because he isn't a very good basketball player.
b. Coach Travis feels Scott is the most valuable player in the game because he scored 26 points.
c. When Scott misses an important shot, he is disappointed, but Coach Travis shows him there are different ways to look at the situation.
d. The Eagles lose the state championship because of Scott, but Coach Travis sees things differently and makes Scott the most valuable player.

7. Why is Scott so upset in this story? Write your response on the lines below. Include evidence from the passage in your response.

____

____

____

____

8. How is Scott's attitude most likely to be different at the beginning of the next basketball season?

a. Scott will be more focused on doing his best than trying to win.
b. Scott will no longer think that winning is a good goal.
c. Scott will become more concerned with having fun than winning.
d. Scott will lose interest in basketball and not care if his team wins.

Refer to the passages "The Talent Show" and "The Tournament" to answer questions 9-10.

9. In what ways are Scott and Megan most similar in these stories?

a. They are both skilled performers.
b. They are both very active athletes.
c. They are both disappointed in themselves.
d. They both have good friends that help them.

10. What general theme is evident in both stories?

a. Winning is important, but it isn't everything.
b. Good friends are the most valuable thing in life.
c. Coaches can offer a good perspective on tough situations.
d. When you try your best, you shouldn't be disappointed in yourself.

Summer Afternoon

Golden sunlight bathes the meadow
In brilliant midday glory.
Slim green pillars bow in homage[1]
To a gentle summer breeze.
Flowers turn their eager faces
Upward to an azure[2] sky.
All is quiet, calm, and peaceful,
Dozing in the pleasant heat.

Just across the sleepy meadow
A lazy stream meanders through,
Sauntering between the banks
Of hardened, sun-baked earth.
Dragonflies flit to and fro
Like scattered thoughts and fleeting dreams.
Bright light glistens on the water
Like sparkling, molten silver.

The meadow rests in tacit glow
As minutes turn to hours.
The sun sinks lower in the sky,
And shadows slowly lengthen.
Daylight, dappled by the trees,
Spreads across the open landscape
Like a dim and dusky cloak,
And—in silence—evening falls.

[1] to honor
[2] blue

Refer to the passage "Summer Afternoon" to answer questions 11-17.

11. What is the meaning of the word *dozing*, as it is used in line 8?

a. Cheering up
b. Singing
c. Working
d. Sleeping

12. Based on lines 1 through 6, what can be concluded about the flowers?

a. The flowers are the only plants that can turn their heads.
b. The flowers were sad until the Sun started shining.
c. The flowers want to face the Sun and receive its sunlight.
d. The flowers do not see the Sun, but they do see the blue sky.

13. Which lines from the poem show that different areas of the environment have different responses to the Sun rising?

a. Slim green pillars bow in homage/To a gentle summer breeze.
b. Just across the sleepy meadow/A lazy stream meanders through,
c. Bright light glistens on the water/Like sparkling, molten silver.
d. Daylight, dappled by the trees,/Spreads across the open landscape

14. What does the line break signify between lines 16 and 17?

a. That the poet is talking about a third area beyond the stream
b. That the tone is changing from cheerful to sorrowful
c. That the last stanza was written by a different poet
d. That the afternoon is ending and the Sun is going down

15. What does the poet's word choice show about the mood in stanzas 1 and 3 compared to the mood in stanza 2?

a. Stanza 2 has an active mood, while stanzas 1 and 3 both have a calm mood.
b. Stanza 2 has an upbeat mood, while stanzas 1 and 3 both have a gloomy mood.
c. Stanza 2 has an exhausted mood, while stanzas 1 and 3 both have a silly mood.
d. Stanza 2 has a fun mood, while stanzas 1 and 3 both have a serious mood.

16. Why does the poet use a compare-and-contrast structure for stanzas 1 and 2?

a. To explain that the events in the meadow caused the events at the stream.
b. To tell why the events in the meadow happened before the events at the stream
c. To show the difference between the events in the meadow and the events at the stream.
d. To present the events in the meadow as the answer for correcting the events at the stream.

17. What is most likely the reason that the poet used a third-person omniscient point of view in this poem?

a. To show what the Sun saw as it shined in the afternoon and set in the evening
b. To describe what happened in different areas and at different times during the day
c. To explain why the dragonflies think the stream and plants in the meadow are lazy
d. To illustrate what can be seen in the meadow in the afternoon and evening

A World of White: The Iditarod Trail

(1) Imagine clinging desperately to your sled as brutal winds batter your body. The path ahead appears and disappears like a mirage, frequently obscured by blowing curtains of snow. You are freezing and sweating at the same time. Your throat burns with thirst, and your body aches with fatigue. You know your dogs must feel it too, so you encourage them to press on to the next checkpoint. All around you, the world is endless, empty, and white. Welcome to the Iditarod Trail.

(2) Alaska's Iditarod Trail is the world's most famous sled dog racing venue. But the trail is older than the sport of sled dog racing. In fact, the Iditarod Trail was first established in the early 1900s, during the Alaskan gold rush. In those days, sled dogs were used for work, hauling thousands of pounds of gold from the landlocked Iditarod to the port of Anchorage. But in faraway Nome, also known for gold, six-year-old George Allen had the idea to put together a race to see whose sled dogs were fastest, and the sport of sled dog racing was born.

(3) Though the Iditarod Trail Race is the most famous race in the sport of sled dog racing, the first race along the trail was actually a race to save lives. In 1925, a diphtheria outbreak began in Nome. To prevent an epidemic that could kill thousands, doctors desperately needed the vaccine serum, but the closest supply of serum was in Anchorage. A train ran from Anchorage to the village of Nenana, but that was still 674 miles from Nome. A cry for help was sent by the doctors, and in the midst of the blizzards and windstorms of January, the call was answered. Twenty brave mushers drove their dogs in a frantic relay, carrying 300,000 bottles of serum from Nenana to Nome. They followed the Iditarod Trail.

(4) Dog sledding, or "mushing," became quite popular after that heroic journey, but by the 1960s, it had lost popularity, and the Iditarod Trail had been largely forgotten. There were a few lovers of mushing, however, who worked tirelessly to reestablish the Iditarod Trail and create a new sled dog race that followed the trail. The first official race was held in 1967 to celebrate the centennial of the purchase of Alaska from Russia. The race involved 58 drivers who mushed 56 miles in two days. This race was a success, but the popularity and future of the Iditarod Trail was still in question.

(5) In March of 1973, the first Anchorage to Nome Iditarod Trail Race was organized and held. This race was much longer than previous races, covering more than 1,000 miles—the entire Iditarod Trail. Thirty-four mushers began the race, but only 22 were able to finish. After the 1973 race, the popularity of the Iditarod Trail finally grew and was firmly established. In 1978, the Iditarod Trail became a National Historic Trail.

(6) The modern Iditarod Trail Race is open to mushers over 18 years old who have qualified in a recognized race of 200 miles or more. For younger mushers between 14 and 18 years old, the Junior Iditarod offers a 130-mile version of the race. Many Junior Iditarod participants go on to compete in the Iditarod Trail Race, as the Junior Iditarod is good practice for the grueling trek of the main race. All mushers must prepare for the race extensively, often for months before. Many mushers run their dogs more than 1,500 miles in preparation, giving them experience in all types of weather and terrain.

(7) To enter the Iditarod Trail Race, participants must pay an entrance fee. Then, they must travel to Anchorage with their dogs. In Anchorage, they attend a mushers' banquet where they are given their racing order numbers. Afterward, all participating dogs are checked by a veterinarian and marked by race officials to prevent participants from switching dogs mid-race, which is not allowed. The dogs are even drug tested at the beginning and at checkpoints throughout the race to prevent cheating! Finally, the sleds and equipment are checked, and participants are ready to start the race.

(8) On the morning of the Iditarod Trail Race, mushers leave Anchorage in their assigned racing order. They are sent out one at a time, at two-minute intervals. For more than a week—sometimes up to three weeks—they travel throughout Alaska, stopping at designated checkpoints along the Iditarod Trail as they make their way to Nome. When all participants have reached Nome, another mushers' banquet is held. Awards are given, and everyone is applauded for their achievement. Win or lose, the mushers know that only the toughest of the tough have what it takes to finish the race and conquer the great Iditarod Trail.

Refer to the passage "A World of White: The Iditarod Trail" to answer questions 18-26.

18. How does the introduction of this passage support the reader's understanding of the Iditarod Trail Race?

a. It shows how intense the race can be for participants.
b. It explains what inspired the race.
c. It describes how hard it is to prepare for the race.
d. It describes the events of the first race on the Iditarod Trail.

19. Why does the author use the simile in the following sentence in paragraph 1?

The path ahead appears and disappears like a mirage, frequently obscured by blowing curtains of snow.

a. To show how heavy the snow is falling
b. To show how difficult it is to see the path
c. To show how cold the mushers must be
d. To show how hard the dogs are running

20. In paragraph 3, which words best convey the feelings of the doctors in Nome in 1925?

a. The words "epidemic" and "diphtheria" show how seriously the doctors took their work.
b. The words "blizzards" and "windstorms" show how scared the doctors were to be in Alaska during winter.
c. The words "brave" and "frantic relay" show how determined the doctors were to cure their patients.
d. The words "desperately" and "cry for help" show how anxious the doctors were to get the serum quickly.

21. Which of the following is the best summary of the history of the Iditarod Trail Race given in paragraphs 4 and 5?

a. After the Iditarod Trail became a National Historic Trail, the race became more popular, and today many mushers participate each year.
b. After a slow start in 1967, the Iditarod Trail Race became firmly established in 1973, and it has grown in popularity.
c. In the first race in 1973, 34 mushers began the race but only 22 finished, proving that the race was too hard.
d. Mushers between 14 and 18 years of age can race in the Junior Iditarod, while those over 18 can participate in the main race if they qualify.

22. This question has two parts. After you answer Part A, answer Part B:

Part A: What is the meaning of the word *epidemic*, used in paragraph 3?

a. A natural disaster
b. Uncontrollable pollution
c. A widespread disease
d. A severe infection

Part B: Which of the following sentences from paragraph 3 helps the reader understand the meaning of *epidemic*?

a. A cry for help was sent by the doctors, and in the midst of the blizzards and windstorms of January, the call was answered.
b. Though the Iditarod Trail Race is the most famous in the sport of sled dog racing, the first race along the trail was actually a race to save lives.
c. In 1925, a diphtheria outbreak began in Nome.
d. A train ran from Anchorage to the village of Nenana, but that was still 674 miles from Nome.

23. What is the author's main purpose in writing this article?

a. To encourage mushers to race on the Iditarod Trail
b. To inform the reader about the 1925 diphtheria outbreak
c. To describe the terrain of Alaska
d. To educate the reader about the Iditarod Trail

24. Which sentence from the passage shows that the sled dogs must also train for the Iditarod Trail Race?

a. In those days, sled dogs were used for work, hauling thousands of pounds of gold from the landlocked Iditarod to the port of Anchorage.
b. Twenty brave mushers drove their dogs in a frantic relay, carrying 300,000 bottles of serum from Nenana to Nome.
c. Many mushers run their dogs more than 1,500 miles in preparation, giving them experience in all types of weather and terrain.
d. Afterward, all participating dogs are checked by a veterinarian and marked by race officials to prevent dog switching mid-race, which is not allowed.

25. Which of the following sentences from the passage supports the central idea that the Iditarod Trail Race has had an eventful history?

a. The path ahead appears and disappears like a mirage, frequently obscured by blowing curtains of snow.
b. Dog sledding, or "mushing," became quite popular after that heroic journey, but by the 1960s, it had lost popularity, and the Iditarod Trail had been largely forgotten.
c. The modern Iditarod Trail Race is open to mushers over 18 years old who have qualified in a recognized race of 200 miles or more.
d. Win or lose, the mushers know that only the toughest of the tough have what it takes to finish the race and conquer the great Iditarod Trail.

26. The supporting details in paragraph 6 support which key idea?

a. Mushers and their dogs should be prepared for the intense conditions they will encounter during the Iditarod Trail Race.
b. There are many stages to preparing for the Iditarod Trail Race since it is one of the most physically-intense competitions.
c. Children and teenagers should not participate in the Iditarod Trail Race because they cannot properly prepare for it.
d. Dog teams must get used to different terrains and weather conditions before beginning the Iditarod Trail Race so they do not get lost.

Extended Response

Your STAAR test will include the following instructions for your extended response question. The response prompts used here are similar to the prompts you will see on the STAAR test.

27. Read the passage "A World of White: The Iditarod Trail." Based on the passage, write a response to the following:

Explain why intense training is needed to compete in the Iditarod Trail Race

Write a well-organized informational composition that uses specific evidence from the passage to support your answer.

Remember to —

- clearly state your controlling idea
- organize your writing
- develop your ideas in detail
- use evidence from the selection in your response
- use correct spelling, capitalization, punctuation, and grammar

Manage your time carefully so that you can —

- review the selection
- plan your response
- write your response
- revise and edit your response

Revising

Christopher wrote the following paper about his daylight saving time. Read the following paper and note the revisions that he should make. Once you have read his paper, answer the questions that follow it.

Daylight Saving Time

(1) Daylight Saving Time (DST) is the portion of the year when people change their clocks so that afternoons have more daylight and mornings have less. (2) Clocks are adjusted forward one hour in the spring and backward one hour in the fall. (3) The main reason for the change is to make better use of daylight.

(4) Daylight Saving Time began with the goal of energy conservation. (5) Benjamin Franklin suggested it as a way to save candles since there would be more daylight and therefore less need for candles when people were awake. (6) It was used during both World Wars to save energy for military needs. (7) Although DST's ability to save energy was one of the main reasons it has been used, it is not clear whether or not DST really saves energy.

(8) Benefits of Daylight Saving Time include having more time for activities that require sunlight after school and work, such as outdoor shopping and sports. (9) It has also been shown that extending DST could bring in a much higher profit for businesses like convenience stores. (10) Public safety may be increased by the use of DST, which could promote public safety. (11) For example, traffic accidents may be reduced when there is additional afternoon sunlight.

(12) Instead, Daylight Saving Time also has some negative impacts. (13) DST can make it difficult to keep time across different areas and time zones. (14) Tools with built-in timekeeping functions, such as watches and medical devices, can be affected if they are not updated when DST begins. (15) Additionally, people interested in agricultural work and evening entertainment have historically disliked DST. (16) Because the Sun rises and sets later, farmers must start working later, and events like concerts and outdoor movies must start later.

(17) DST can also affect health, both positively and negatively. (18) It also impacts sunlight exposure. (19) This can be good because it helps people take in more vitamin D. (20) Sun exposure is one major source of vitamin D, so it can be beneficial. (21) However, it can also be bad because too much sun exposure can negatively affect people's health. (22) DST may also disrupt sleep by making it more difficult for people to go to sleep early.

(23) Today, Daylight Saving Time is used by more than one billion people in about 70 countries. (24) DST is generally not used in countries near the equator because sunrise times do not vary much there. (25) Asian and African countries also usually do not observe it. (26) Some countries, such as Brazil, observe it in only some regions. (27) Except for Arizona and Hawaii, all states in the US observe DST.

28. Sentence 10 currently contains repeated information. On the lines below, write a revised version of sentence 10 that is not repetitive.

____

____

____

29. Sentence 12 could be improved with a more effective transition. Which of the following transition phrases should be used instead of *Instead* in sentence 12?

a. Because of this
b. Furthermore
c. However
d. Likewise

30. Another sentence is needed to support sentence 17. Which of the following sentences should be added after this sentence?

a. It is important to check with one's doctor before spending a long time outside.
b. There are so many ways to stay active during the day, either indoors or outdoors.
c. The way the day is spent and the things people eat also impact health.
d. It provides more afternoon sunlight, which allows people to get exercise.

31. Which of the following sentences is repetitive and should be removed from the fifth paragraph?

a. Sentence 17
b. Sentence 18
c. Sentence 20
d. Sentence 21

32. Which of the following sentences should be added after sentence 27 to improve the passage's conclusion?

a. If you live in an area that does not observe Daylight Saving Time, consider taking action to promote DST near your home.
b. Whether you observe Daylight Saving Time or not, this practice continues to have an impact on people across the world.
c. Remember that Daylight Saving Time affects more than a person's sleep schedule; it can also impact the rest of a person's life.
d. Arizona and Hawaii used to observe Daylight Saving Time, but both states decided to stop observing it in the 1960s.

Jamie wrote the following narrative about a family's vacation. Read the following paper and note the revisions that she should make. Once you have read her paper, answer the questions that follow it.

The Washington Family Vacation

(1) Mr. and Mrs. Washington, their dog, and their kids, Arlo and Ella, piled into the family car. (2) They were on their way to visit Mr. Washington's cousin, Lucy, at her home by Lake Tahoe. (3) In the car, they were surrounded by clothes, fishing equipment, and presents for Lucy and Lucy's family. (4) Penny, the dog, sat in the seat next to Ella. (5) Since Ella was an avid painter, they brought her backpack with all her paints and brushes so she could do paintings of the lake.

(6) They decided to stop for lunch when for about two hours they had been driving. (7) Mrs. Washington exited the highway and stopped by a shady tree.

(8) As they got out of the car, Mr. Washington grabbed a pen so he could fill in a crossword puzzle. (9) The pen leaked and left a stripe of blue ink on his hand, which he absentmindedly wiped on his white t-shirt. (10) Everybody got out of the car, put down blankets to sit on, and got out the sandwiches and drinks. (11) Penny ate all her food and laid down on the blanket for a nap in the sun. (12) Arlo and Ella then decided to climb the tree. (13) Ella kept her backpack on when she climbed the tree with Arlo.

(14) Under the tree, Mr. Washington was tired, so he laid down next to Penny, who was dreaming and kicking in her sleep. (15) He pulled his hat over his eyes and fell asleep. (16) Mrs. Washington enjoyed the quiet and read her book as she ate her sandwich. (17) Suddenly, a wasp flew by and startled her, and she dropped her sandwich on Mr. Washington. (18) Mustard from her sandwich spilled on his shirt. (19) Penny jumped on Mr. Washington with her paws covered in tomato juice.

(20) In the tree, Ella was getting crackers out of her backpack when she looked down to see the commotion. (21) She laughed so hard at what she saw that she dropped her backpack with the paints in it. (22) The green paint did not have its lid screwed on tightly, and it landed on Mr. Washington's shirt next to the red, yellow, and blue marks.

(23) Mr. Washington was wide awake now and looked with surprise at his shirt. (24) Everyone else was laughing. (25) Arlo then got sad that he hadn't helped color his dad's shirt. (26) He found a plum in the cooler and looked at his dad questioningly. (27) Mr. Washington sighed and nodded at Arlo. (28) Arlo bit the fruit and rubbed the juice on his dad's shirt.

(29) When they got to Lake Tahoe, Lucy's four-year-old daughter came to the door and squealed when she saw them. (30) She yelled to her mom, "Mom, Uncle Rainbow is here!" (31) And that's what she has called him ever since.

33. Sentence 6 is unclear. Which of the following is the best revision of sentence 6?

a. They had been driving for about two hours when they decided to stop for lunch.
b. For about two hours, they decided to stop for lunch when they had been driving.
c. When they had been for lunch for about two hours, they decided to stop driving.
d. They decided to stop driving for when lunch they had been for about two hours.

34. Sentence 13 repeats an idea from sentence 12. Which phrase should be removed from sentence 13 to remove the repetition?

a. Ella kept her
b. backpack on
c. climbed the tree
d. with Arlo

35. A supporting detail should be added after sentence 18. Which of the following sentences would be best to add there?

a. The mustard was a bright yellow and stained Mr. Washington's shirt.
b. She gasped and woke up Penny, who jumped into the tomato salad.
c. The wasp quickly flew away and, thankfully, did not sting anyone.
d. If Penny had been awake, she would have caught the mustard as it spilled.

36. Which of the following sentences should be added after sentence 22 to improve the transition from the fifth paragraph to the sixth paragraph?

a. Mrs. Washington was upset that the shirt was stained.
b. Mr. Washington thought the marks were hilarious.
c. His shirt looked like the beginning of a rainbow.
d. Ella was afraid she would get in trouble for the paint spill.

Editing

Allison is writing an essay about the history of Nebraska. Read the following paragraphs from the body of Allison's essay and look for errors that she needs to correct. Once you have read the paragraphs, answer the questions that follow them.

Life in Nebraska

(1) Life as a pioneer in nebraska was not easy. (2) Most families farmed and lived in sod houses or log cabins. (3) They didn't have electricity or running water. (4) These pioneers faced many challenges, and these challenges were especially hard for the children. (5) Since prairie farmers often could not afford to hire adult helpers they relied on their children to help.

(6) Children arose early, while it was still dark, to begin their chores. (7) Some chores even had to be done before breakfast! (8) Different seasons called for different chores. (9) Boys learned to plant and harvest crops. (10) They hunted and fished to provide food for the family. (11) Sometimes they gathered cow or buffalo chips to use as fuel for the fire. (12) Girls helped with gathering eggs, cooking, cleaning the house, mending clothes and socks, and taking care of the younger children. (13) Since these children had to help their parents with work around the farm, they had very different childhoods than today's children has.

37. Which change would correct the mistake in sentence 1?

a. Change *as* to *with*.
b. Add a comma after *pioneer*.
c. Change *nebraska* to *Nebraska*.
d. Change *was* to *were*.

38. Which change would correct the mistake in sentence 4?

a. Change *faced* to *face*.
b. Remove the comma after *challenges*.
c. Change *especially* to *especially*.
d. No change is needed in sentence 4.

39. Which change would correct the mistake in sentence 5?

a. Change *prairie* to *Prairie*.
b. Add a comma after *helpers*.
c. Change *they* to *them*.
d. Change *relied* to *relies*.

40. Which change would correct the mistake in sentence 13?

a. Change *their* to *there*.
b. Remove the comma after *farm*.
c. Change *children* to *childs*.
d. Change *has* to *have*.

Keith is writing an informational essay about the Olympics. Read the following paragraphs from the body of his essay and look for errors that Keith needs to correct. Once you have read the paragraphs, answer the questions that follow.

The History of the Olympics

(1) Today, the Olympics still happened every four years, but they are split into the Summer and Winter Games. (2) The top athletes, men and women alike, compete for medals. (3) Gold is awarded for first place, silver is awarded for second place, and bronze is awarded for third place. (4) Furthermore, the Olympics feature both solo events and team events. (5) An average of 200 nations and over 10,000 athletes compete at the Olympics today. (6) The Olympics are run by the International Olympic Committee, also called the ioc, who make many decisions that allow the Olympic Games to continue and change.

(7) The Olympic flame still burns. (8) It is lit at the site of the ancient Olympic Games in Greece several months before the opening ceremonies. (9) A parabolic mirror is used to focus the Sun's rays and light the torch. (10) Then, runners carry the torch around Greece, passing it to the next person like runners in a relay race. (11) Slowly, the flame is transferred to runners in the host country. (12) Until 2008, the torch was carried through many countries before reaching the host, but today it is given directly to the country, where the Olympic Games are being held. (13) The final runner lights the Olympic Flame with the torch. (14) Just like in ancient times the flame stays lit until the games are complete.

41. Which change would correct the mistake in sentence 1?

a. Remove the comma after *Today*.
b. Change *happened* to *happen*.
c. Change *but* to *so*.
d. Change *Games* to *games*.

42. Which change would correct the mistake in sentence 6?

a. Change *by* to *with*.
b. Change *ioc* to *IOC*.
c. Change *allow* to *allows*.
d. No change is needed in sentence 6.

43. Which word should be used in place of *Slowly* in sentence 11?

__________, the flame is transferred to runners in the host country.

Finally
However
Clearly
Previously

44. Which change would correct the mistake in sentence 12?

a. Change *Until* to *After*.
b. Change *carried* to *carreed*.
c. Remove the comma after *country*.
d. Change *are* to *were*.

45. Which change would correct the mistake in sentence 14?

a. Change *ancient times* to *Ancient Times.*
b. Add a comma after *times.*
c. Change *stays* to *stay.*
d. Change *are* to *will be.*

Answer Key and Explanations for Test #2

Reading

1. A: TEKS Standard (6.7)(A)

The main theme of the story is about the support that real friendship provides. Megan's friends comfort her after her performance, leading to Megan's conclusion in paragraph 16 that everything will be okay because of her supportive friends. While the other three answer choices did occur in the story, they are simply supportive details rather than the main idea.

2. B: TEKS Standard (6.5)(F)

Kaylee points out that Megan should focus on what she did sing rather than what she didn't sing because the part of the song she was able to sing was great. Kaylee did not make a joke about Megan's performance (A). Kaylee also didn't want to simply distract Megan from (C) or help her forget (D) the fact that she didn't finish the song; she wanted Megan to focus on the good aspects of her performance.

3. D: TEKS Standard (6.8)(A)

Realistic fiction is a genre in which the events of the story did not actually happen but could have potentially happened in real life. The events in this story could have taken place in real life. Choices A, B, and C are incorrect because they describe aspects that could be in any story, not just realistic fiction.

4. B: TEKS Standard (6.7)(C)

Paragraph 2 describes the moment Megan forgot the words to the song and ran backstage. This is the point where the story's conflict begins. Choice A is incorrect because Megan does not mention thinking she would win the talent show in the paragraph. Choice C is incorrect because there was no mention of Megan wanting to avoid her friends. Choice D is incorrect because it is never explained why Megan forgot the words to the song.

5. D: TEKS Standard (6.9)(D)

A metaphor is a nonliteral comparison between two things. Scott is compared to a statue in the metaphor in paragraph 4 to demonstrate how dismayed he was that his team lost the game. Choice A is incorrect because the crowd did not alarm Scott. Choice B is incorrect because Scott was not proud of his performance, as he had missed the game's winning shot. Choice C is incorrect because Scott was no longer focused, as the game had already ended.

6. C: TEKS Standard (6.6)(D)

This choice effectively sums up the main points expressed within the story. Choice A is incorrect because Scott's lack of skill isn't implied within the story at all. Choices B and D focus more on supporting details than the main ideas, so they are incorrect.

7. TEKS Standard (6.5)(F)

Scott thinks he is responsible for the fact that his team lost. At the end of paragraph 3, Scott connects his missed shot to his team's loss. Throughout paragraphs 6 and 7, Scott experiences confusion. This is because he does not understand how he was named the most valuable player since he missed the last shot and believes the Eagles's loss is his fault.

8. A: TEKS Standard (6.5)(C)

In paragraphs 10-12, Coach Travis helps Scott understand that, as long as he did his best, winning doesn't matter. Choice B is incorrect because, although Scott may be less focused on winning, it is still important to him. Choice C is incorrect because the story's focus was on the effort Scott put into winning, not on how much fun he had. Choice D is incorrect because the story clearly shows that winning is important to Scott.

9. C: TEKS Standard (6.5)(E)

Scott gets disappointed in himself for missing the winning shot, while Megan gets disappointed in herself for forgetting the words to her song. Choices A and B are incorrect because Scott is not a performer (A), and Megan is not an athlete (B). Choice D is incorrect because Scott's story does not mention his relationship with his friends.

10. D: TEKS Standard (6.5)(E)

Both Scott and Megan show disappointment with themselves within their stories. Choice A is incorrect because, although both characters had a desire to win, that was not the main theme in either story. Choice B is incorrect because friendship was not a theme in Scott's story. Choice C is incorrect because Megan did not have a coach in her story.

11. D: TEKS Standard (6.2)(B)

Dozing is another word for *sleeping*, so choice D is correct. This meaning is supported by the other descriptions in the poem. In line 9, the speaker says that the meadow is sleepy. Additionally, the words *gentle*, *quiet*, *calm*, and *peaceful* in stanza 1 show that there is not much activity in the meadow. The poem does not suggest that the things in the meadow are upset, gloomy, or sad. This shows that the poem does not support the idea that dozing would mean *cheering up*, so choice A is incorrect. The meadow is described as quiet, so the things in it would not be singing. Therefore, choice B is incorrect. There are no details in the poem that suggest that the things in the meadow have tasks to complete or are working, so choice C is incorrect.

12. C: TEKS Standard (6.5)(H)

When the Sun is high in the sky and light falls on the meadow, lines 5 and 6 say that the "flowers turn their eager faces" toward the Sun. *Eager* means that someone or something is excited or ready for something. This supports the idea that the flowers are glad to face the Sun and that they want to do so. Choice C is correct. Lines 1 through 6 only mention one other plant: the grass. While the grass does not turn, this does not mean that other, unmentioned plants cannot turn their heads. Choice A is incorrect. The flowers were facing the ground before the Sun came up. However, the poem does not suggest that the flowers were sad. The speaker is simply describing the flowers sitting up and opening when the Sun comes up. Choice B is incorrect. The poem says that the Sun "bathes the meadow," which means that its light covers the whole meadow. The poem also does not mention anything that would block the flowers' view of the Sun, so choice D is incorrect.

13. B: TEKS Standard (6.6)(C)

The poem describes what happens in the meadow and the area near the stream during the middle of the day. The meadow and area near the stream are different areas of the environment. Choice B shows that, in response to the Sun rising to its peak in the sky, the meadow is sleepy and the stream is lazily moving. These lines show that the things in the meadow are still and calm, and the things near the stream are active and moving. This means choice B is correct. The lines in choice A simply describe the grass bowing to the breeze. This describes one area and its response, so choice A is incorrect. The lines in choice C only describe the stream, so choice C is also incorrect. The lines in choice D describe what happens when the Sun descends. They do not describe a response to the Sun rising, so choice D is incorrect.

14. D: TEKS Standard (6.8)(B)

Line breaks are often used to show a change in idea or focus in a poem. Stanzas 1 and 2 describe what happens in the middle of the day when the Sun is high in the sky. Stanza 3 describes what happens in the evening when the Sun is going down. This means that the line break between the stanzas signifies that time has passed, so choice D is correct. The third stanza mentions the meadow in line 17, and it does not introduce a new area, so choice A is incorrect. The tone does not become sorrowful in stanza 3, so choice B is incorrect. One poet wrote the entire poem, and there is nothing to signal that the writer has changed. This means that choice C is incorrect.

15. A: TEKS Standard (6.9)(F)

Stanza 2 describes the stream moving through the area, the dragonflies quickly moving around, and the water sparkling. Stanza 2 also includes words like "sauntering," "flit," "scattered," "fleeting," and "sparkling." These elements and words create an active mood in stanza 2. Stanzas 1 and 3 describe plants that stay in their places, enjoy the rising sun, and rest as it sets. These stanzas have a calm mood. The plants in the meadow are not described as being gloomy or serious. They are glad and restful, so choices B and D are incorrect. The stream and dragonflies in stanza 2 are not exhausted, so choice C is incorrect.

16. C: TEKS Standard (6.9)(B)

Stanza 1 describes the meadow during midday, and stanza 2 describes the area near the stream during midday. The events that happen in these areas are different, so the poet contrasts them by describing them in different stanzas. This means choice C is correct. The events in the meadow and near the stream are both caused by the Sun rising, so choice A is incorrect. The events in the meadow and the events near the stream happen at the same time. This means that choice B is incorrect. There is not a problem created by the events near the stream, so choice D is incorrect.

17. B: TEKS Standard (6.9)(E)

The use of a third-person omniscient narrator allowed the poet to describe events that occurred in different places at the same time. Choice B is correct. The Sun is not the narrator of the poem, and the poem does not describe the environment from the Sun's perspective, so choice A is incorrect. The dragonflies' thoughts are not described in the poem, so choice C is incorrect. The second stanza of the poem describes what happens outside of the meadow. Also, a first-person narrator could describe what can be seen in the meadow during the afternoon and evening. This makes choice D incorrect.

18. D: TEKS Standard (6.8)(Dii)

The introductory paragraph describes the experience of a participant in the Iditarod Trail Race, which supports the reader's understanding of the conditions the racers endure. This makes choice A correct. Choices B and C are incorrect, as the inspiration of the race is described in paragraph 3, and preparation techniques are described in paragraph 5. The passage does not indicate that paragraph 1 is describing the first Iditarod Trail Race, so choice D is incorrect.

19. B: TEKS Standard (6.9)(D)

The author compares the path appearing and disappearing to a mirage. This indicates how difficult it is to see the path. Choice A is incorrect because, although the author describes how hard the snow is falling, no comparison is being made, so it is not a part of the simile. Choices C and D are incorrect because there is no mention of how cold it is or how hard the dogs are running.

20. D: TEKS Standard (6.9)(F)

The words "desperately" and "cry for help" demonstrate the urgency of the situation and how anxious the doctors were to get it resolved. The words in the other answer choices do not effectively indicate how the doctors were feeling.

21. B: TEKS Standard (6.6)(D)

This is the best summary for paragraphs 4 and 5 as it effectively sums up the main points the author was trying to make. The other answer choices are incorrect because they only state supporting details provided within the paragraphs.

22. TEKS Standard (6.2)(B)

Part A: C: The previous sentence mentions a "diphtheria outbreak," which shows the reader that the passage is describing a disease that has spread wildly. Choices A and B are incorrect, as the paragraph is talking about a disease outbreak, not a natural disaster or pollution. Choice D is incorrect because the word "epidemic" is describing how much the disease has spread, not its severity.

Part B: C: Diphtheria is a disease, and an outbreak is when a very contagious disease spreads to a lot of people in an area. The doctors wanted to prevent an epidemic that the diphtheria outbreak could have caused. This shows that the sentence in choice C helps the reader understand the definition of *epidemic*. Choice A is incorrect because it tells the reader that the doctors needed help, and despite the weather, they received it. This sentence does mention doctors, but it does not show that the doctors were trying to prevent the spread of a disease. Choice B is incorrect because it states that the trail was first used to save lives. This sentence does not mention a disease or the spread of illness. Choice D is incorrect because it tells the reader why it was difficult to get to Nome. It does not show the reader what the problem in Nome was.

23. D: TEKS Standard (6.9)(A)

This passage gives the reader information on the Iditarod Trail. Choice A is incorrect because, although information is given on how to participate in races on the trail, no encouragement is provided. Choices B and C are incorrect because they are just minor supporting details.

24. C: TEKS Standard (6.6)(C)

Choice C is correct because it describes the preparation that sled dogs go through in order to get ready for the race. Choices A and B are incorrect because they only explain what the dogs were used for before the creation of the race. Choice D is incorrect because it only describes how the dogs are evaluated to ensure they are medically ready to participate in the race.

25. B: TEKS Standard (6.8)(Di)

They key words "heroic journey" help to support the idea that the history of the Iditarod Trail Race was an eventful one. The remaining answer choices focus on other details of the trail, such as its harsh conditions (A and D) and the requirements one must meet to participate in the race (C) instead of the trail's history.

26. A: TEKS Standard (6.5)(G)

Paragraph 6 describes how mushers and their dogs run more than 1,500 miles in preparation for the race. It also states that they practice running in all kinds of weather and terrain. This evidence supports the key idea that mushers and their dogs should be prepared for the intense conditions of the Iditarod Trail.

Extended Response

27. TEKS Standard (6.11)(B)

Please use the rubric below to make sure your response meets these criteria. Try to have a friend or family member grade your response for you or take a break after writing your response and return to grade it yourself with fresh eyes.

Below is an excerpt of the STAAR Grades 6-EII Informational Writing Rubric.

<table>
<tr><th>Score Point</th><th>Organization and Development of Ideas</th></tr>
<tr><td>3</td><td><ul><li>Controlling idea/Thesis is clear and fully developed
The controlling idea/thesis is clearly identifiable. The focus is consistent throughout, creating a response that is unified and easy to follow.</li><li>Organization is effective
A purposeful structure that includes an effective introduction and conclusion is evident. The organizational structure is appropriate and effectively supports the development of the controlling idea/thesis. The sentences, paragraphs, or ideas are logically connected in purposeful and highly effective ways.</li><li>Evidence is specific, well chosen, and relevant
The response includes relevant text-based evidence that is clearly explained and consistently supports and develops the controlling idea/thesis. For pairs in grades 6 through EII, evidence is drawn from both texts. The response reflects a thorough understanding of the writing purpose.</li><li>Expression of ideas is clear and effective
The writer's word choice is specific, purposeful, and enhances the response. Almost all sentences and phrases are effectively crafted to convey the writer's ideas and contribute to the overall quality of the response and the clarity of the message.</li></ul></td></tr>
<tr><th>Score Point</th><th>Conventions</th></tr>
<tr><td>2</td><td>Student writing demonstrates consistent command of grade-level-appropriate conventions, including correct:<ul><li>sentence construction</li><li>punctuation</li><li>capitalization</li><li>grammar</li><li>spelling</li></ul>The response has few errors, but those errors do not impact the clarity of the writing.</td></tr>
</table>

Revising

28. TEKS Standard (6.10)(C)

Sentence 10 currently states that public safety could be increased twice. A revised version of this sentence should only state this idea once. The revision may be similar to the following sentence: Public safety may be increased by the use of DST. The new sentence must have the same meaning as this sentence. The new sentence should also be complete, grammatically correct, and clear. It should state the information in an order that makes sense and is easy to read.

29. C: TEKS Standard (6.10)(Bi)

Sentences 8 through 11 in paragraph 3 describe the benefits of Daylight Saving Time. Sentence 12 states that DST can have negative impacts. The information in sentence 12 is contrasted against the information from the previous paragraph. The transition at the beginning of sentence 12 should show this relationship. *Instead* means that one possibility is replaced by another possibility. This is not the relationship the transition should show. *However* shows that while one statement is true, a contrasting statement is also true. This means that *however* is a good transition for sentence 12, so choice C is correct. Choice A is incorrect since the positive effects of DST do not cause the negative effects of DST. Choices B and D are incorrect because they do not show that there is a contrast between the positive and negative effects of DST.

30. D: TEKS Standard (6.10)(Bii)

Choice D supports sentence 17 by giving an example of how DST can have a positive effect on someone's health. Choices A, B, and C are incorrect because they are not specifically related to DST, so they do not support sentence 17. Each of these statements is related to sunlight and health. However, these statements would also be true outside of Daylight Saving Time.

31. C: TEKS Standard (6.10)(Bii)

Choice C is correct because sentence 20 repeats the ideas in sentence 19. Choice A is incorrect because sentence 17 is the topic sentence and it tells the reader what the paragraph is about. Choice B is incorrect because sentence 18 contains an important detail. It also supports the information in sentence 17. Choice D is incorrect because sentence 21 gives an example of how Daylight Saving Time can negatively impact a person's health. This also supports the information in sentence 17.

32. B: TEKS Standard (6.10)(Bi)

Choice B is correct because it is related to the overall topic of the passage. It also does not focus on one detail, and it summarizes the ideas described in the passage. Choice A is incorrect because it changes the purpose of the passage. This passage is meant to provide information about Daylight Saving Time, and it does this by including the positive and negative effects of DST. However, the passage is not meant to persuade the reader. The sentence in choice A would only be appropriate if this passage were meant to persuade the reader to promote DST. Choice C is incorrect because it focuses on details from the passage. It also tells the reader to do something, which is more appropriate for a persuasive passage than an informational one. Choice D is incorrect because it tells the reader new information. The concluding sentence of a paper should not tell the reader details that are not already present in the passage.

33. A: TEKS Standard (6.10)(C)

Sentence 6 says that the Washingtons decided to stop for lunch and that they had been driving for two hours. The sentence should make it clear that after the Washingtons had been driving for two hours, they decided to stop for lunch. Choice A is correct because it clearly states this information. Choice B is incorrect because it suggests that the Washingtons took two hours to decide to stop for lunch. Choice C is incorrect because it is grammatically incorrect. It also seems to say that the Washingtons decided to stop driving after they had been having lunch for two hours. Choice D is also grammatically incorrect. It also seems to have the same meaning as choice C, which is incorrect.

34. D: TEKS Standard (6.10)(C)

Sentence 12 says that Arlo and Ella decided to climb the tree. Sentence 13 is meant to tell the reader that Ella had her backpack on when she climbed the tree. Since sentence 12 says that Ella and Arlo climbed the tree, choice D is correct. The idea that Arlo also climbed the tree does not need to be stated again in sentence 12. Choice A is incorrect because without the words "Ella kept her," the sentence would be incomplete. Choice B is incorrect because without the phrase "backpack on," the sentence would have a different meaning, and it would be unclear. Choice C is incorrect because the sentence would not make sense without the words "climbed the tree."

35. B: TEKS Standard (6.10)(Bii)

Sentence 18 says that mustard from Mrs. Washington's sandwich fell on Mr. Washington's shirt. Sentence 19 says that Penny jumped on Mr. Washington and that her paws were covered in tomato juice. The passage does not explain what happened in between these events. It also does not explain how the tomato juice got on Penny's paws. Choice B is correct because it shows that Mrs. Washington woke up Penny, who then stepped on some tomatoes. This sentence shows the connection between sentences 18 and 19. Choices A and C are incorrect because they do not help the reader understand the passage. They also do not provide the missing information. Choice D is incorrect because this does not explain the event that occurred between sentences 18 and 19.

36. C: TEKS Standard (6.10)(Bi)

Throughout the story, things have been smudged onto Mr. Washington's shirt. Sentence 22 says that there are now four colors on his white shirt: green, red, yellow, and blue. Choice C is correct because it helps the reader see that these smudges have landed in a way that looks like a rainbow. This sentence also helps the reader understand why Lucy's daughter calls Mr. Washington "Uncle Rainbow" at the end of the sixth paragraph. Choice A is incorrect because sentence 24 shows that Mrs. Washington thought the stains were funny. Choice B is incorrect because Mr. Washington is still asleep at this point in the story. Additionally, in sentence 27, Mr. Washington sighs when Arlo wants to add more color to the shirt. Choice B does not support the other details in the passage. Choice D is incorrect because Ella laughs at the spill. The idea that Ella would get in trouble does not support the later events in the passage.

Editing

37. C: TEKS Standard (6.10)(Dvii)

Nebraska is the name of a state in America. It is a proper noun, so it should be capitalized, which means choice C is correct. The sentence is describing how the pioneers lived. It is not describing the people who lived with pioneers, so choice A is incorrect. There is no need to add a comma after *pioneer*, so choice B is incorrect. *Was* is a singular verb, and *were* is a plural verb. Since *life* is a singular noun, it should be used with a singular verb. *Was* is the correct verb to use in sentence 1, so choice D is incorrect.

38. D: TEKS Standard (6.10)(D)

There are no errors in spelling or grammar in sentence 4, so choice D is correct. Sentence 4 is written in the past tense. *Faced* is a past tense verb. When it is used without any helping verbs, like in sentence 4, *face* is a present tense verb. *Faced* is used correctly in sentence 4, so choice A is incorrect. The comma after *challenges* is used to link two independent clauses together. The comma in sentence 4 is needed, so choice B is incorrect. In *especially*, the root word is *special*, and the suffix is *-ly*. There is no need to drop the final letter from the root word *special*. This means that when the suffix *-ly* is added, the word will contain two *ls*. *Especially* is spelled correctly, so choice C is incorrect.

39. B: TEKS Standard (6.10)(Dviii)

Sentence 5 is a complex sentence. It is made of one dependent clause and one independent clause. When a dependent clause comes before an independent clause, it must end with a comma. "Since prairie farmers often could not afford to hire adult helpers" is a dependent clause because it begins with *since*, a subordinating conjunction. This clause should end with a comma, so choice B is correct. The word *prairie* is not referring to a specific place, so it is not a proper noun. Choice A is incorrect. *They* is a subjective pronoun. In sentence 5, it is used as the subject of the independent clause. *They* is used correctly, so choice C is correct. Sentence 5 is written in the past tense. *Relied* is a past tense verb, so it is used correctly in sentence 5. Choice D is incorrect.

40. D: TEKS Standard (6.10)(Di)

Has is a singular verb, and *have* is a plural verb. *Children* is a plural noun, so it should be used with a plural verb. *Has* should be changed to *have* in sentence 13, so choice D is correct. *Their* is a possessive pronoun. In sentence 13, *their* is used to show that the parents belong to the children. The word is used correctly, so choice A is incorrect. The word *farm* is the last word in a dependent clause. In sentence 13, the dependent clause comes before the independent clause. This means that the dependent clause should end in a comma, so choice B is incorrect. The word *child* is an irregular noun because, in its plural form, it is not written using an *-s* or *-es*. *Children* is the plural form of *child*, so choice C is incorrect.

41. B: TEKS Standard (6.10)(Dii)

Sentence 1 is about events that are happening today, so it is in the present tense. *Happened* is a past tense verb, and *happen* is a present tense verb. *Happen* is the better verb to use in this sentence because it is in the present tense, so choice B is correct. The word *today* is used in sentence 1 as an introduction. Usually, when words are used in this way, they are followed by a comma. The comma after *today* is acceptable, so choice A is incorrect. The conjunction *but* is used to show contrast, and the conjunction *so* is used to show an effect. This sentence is saying that even though the Olympics are still happening today, they are different than they were long ago. The correct conjunction to use is *but* since it contrasts the old and current Olympics. Choice C is incorrect. The Summer and Winter Games are specific events. The word *Games* is part of the title for both events, so it should be capitalized. Choice D is incorrect.

42. B: TEKS Standard (6.10)(Dvii)

Initialisms are abbreviations that are created using the first letter of each word in a title. Each letter in an initialism is capitalized if the word it represents is capitalized in the title. All of the words in International Olympic Committee are capitalized, so its initialism should be IOC. This means that choice B is correct. The IOC is the group that runs the Olympics. If *by* were changed to *with* in sentence 6, the meaning of the sentence would change. Instead, it would say that The Olympics and the IOC run the games together. This is not true, so choice A is incorrect. *Allow* is a plural verb, and *allows* is a singular verb. *Decisions* is a plural noun, so it should be used with a plural verb like *allow*. Choice C is incorrect. Choice D is incorrect because sentence 6 contained an error in capitalization.

43. Finally: TEKS Standard (6.10)(Diii)

This sentence should describe when the flame is given to the runners in the host country. While the process does take a long time, the word *slowly* is not the best choice for sentence 12. *Slowly* does not show when in the process the host country receives the flame. The word *finally* shows that the flame is given to the host country near the end of the race. *Finally* is the correct choice because it gives the reader needed information and helps clarify the sentence's meaning. *However* would not make sense in the blank because it would suggest that the flame is not expected to go to the host country. Using *clearly* in the blank does not help the reader understand how or when the flame is given to the host country, so it is incorrect. Using *previously* in the blank would mean that this process only happened in the past. However, the sentence is in present tense, so *previously* is not the correct choice for this sentence.

44. C: TEKS Standard (6.10)(Dv)

In sentence 12, the word *where* connects important information to the rest of the sentence. The information is necessary, so it should not be separated from the rest of the sentence. The comma between *country* and *where* should be removed, so choice C is correct. Changing *until* to *after* would change the meaning of the sentence. Since the torch was given directly to the host country in the years leading up to 2008, not after 2008, *until* is the correct word to use at the beginning of the sentence. Choice A is incorrect. When the suffix *-ed* is added to a word ending in *y*, the *y* is usually changed to an *i*. When the suffix *-ed* is added to *carry*, the resulting word is *carried*. *Carreed* is a misspelling of *carried*, so choice B is incorrect. This sentence is written in the present tense. *Are* is a present tense verb, and *were* is a past tense verb. *Are* is the correct verb to use in this sentence, so choice D is incorrect.

45. B: TEKS Standard (6.10)(Dviii)

The phrase "Just like in ancient times" is a prepositional phrase. When a longer prepositional phrase is used at the beginning of a sentence, it should end with a comma. This makes choice B correct. The phrase "ancient times" does not refer to a specific time period or era. This means that it is not a proper noun, so it should not be capitalized. Choice A is incorrect. *Stays* is a singular verb, while *stay* is a plural verb. Since *flame* is a singular noun, it should be used with *stays*, a singular verb. This means that choice c is incorrect. This sentence is in the present tense. *Are* is a present tense verb, and *will be* is a future tense verb phrase. *Are* matches the tense of sentence 14, so choice D is incorrect.

Practice Test #3

To take this additional STAAR practice test, visit our online resources page:
mometrix.com/resources719/staarg6rla

How to Overcome Test Anxiety

Just the thought of taking a test is enough to make most people a little nervous. A test is an important event that can have a long-term impact on your future, so it's important to take it seriously and it's natural to feel anxious about performing well. But just because anxiety is normal, that doesn't mean that it's helpful in test taking, or that you should simply accept it as part of your life. Anxiety can have a variety of effects. These effects can be mild, like making you feel slightly nervous, or severe, like blocking your ability to focus or remember even a simple detail.

If you experience test anxiety—whether severe or mild—it's important to know how to beat it. To discover this, first you need to understand what causes test anxiety.

Causes of Test Anxiety

While we often think of anxiety as an uncontrollable emotional state, it can actually be caused by simple, practical things. One of the most common causes of test anxiety is that a person does not feel adequately prepared for their test. This feeling can be the result of many different issues such as poor study habits or lack of organization, but the most common culprit is time management. Starting to study too late, failing to organize your study time to cover all of the material, or being distracted while you study will mean that you're not well prepared for the test. This may lead to cramming the night before, which will cause you to be physically and mentally exhausted for the test. Poor time management also contributes to feelings of stress, fear, and hopelessness as you realize you are not well prepared but don't know what to do about it.

Other times, test anxiety is not related to your preparation for the test but comes from unresolved fear. This may be a past failure on a test, or poor performance on tests in general. It may come from comparing yourself to others who seem to be performing better or from the stress of living up to expectations. Anxiety may be driven by fears of the future—how failure on this test would affect your educational and career goals. These fears are often completely irrational, but they can still negatively impact your test performance.

Elements of Test Anxiety

As mentioned earlier, test anxiety is considered to be an emotional state, but it has physical and mental components as well. Sometimes you may not even realize that you are suffering from test anxiety until you notice the physical symptoms. These can include trembling hands, rapid heartbeat, sweating, nausea, and tense muscles. Extreme anxiety may lead to fainting or vomiting. Obviously, any of these symptoms can have a negative impact on testing. It is important to recognize them as soon as they begin to occur so that you can address the problem before it damages your performance.

The mental components of test anxiety include trouble focusing and inability to remember learned information. During a test, your mind is on high alert, which can help you recall information and stay focused for an extended period of time. However, anxiety interferes with your mind's natural processes, causing you to blank out, even on the questions you know well. The strain of testing during anxiety makes it difficult to stay focused, especially on a test that may take several hours. Extreme anxiety can take a huge mental toll, making it difficult not only to recall test information but even to understand the test questions or pull your thoughts together.

Effects of Test Anxiety

Test anxiety is like a disease—if left untreated, it will get progressively worse. Anxiety leads to poor performance, and this reinforces the feelings of fear and failure, which in turn lead to poor performances on subsequent tests. It can grow from a mild nervousness to a crippling condition. If allowed to progress, test anxiety can have a big impact on your schooling, and consequently on your future.

Test anxiety can spread to other parts of your life. Anxiety on tests can become anxiety in any stressful situation, and blanking on a test can turn into panicking in a job situation. But fortunately, you don't have to let anxiety rule your testing and determine your grades. There are a number of relatively simple steps you can take to move past anxiety and function normally on a test and in the rest of life.

Physical Steps for Beating Test Anxiety

While test anxiety is a serious problem, the good news is that it can be overcome. It doesn't have to control your ability to think and remember information. While it may take time, you can begin taking steps today to beat anxiety.

Just as your first hint that you may be struggling with anxiety comes from the physical symptoms, the first step to treating it is also physical. Rest is crucial for having a clear, strong mind. If you are tired, it is much easier to give in to anxiety. But if you establish good sleep habits, your body and mind will be ready to perform optimally, without the strain of exhaustion. Additionally, sleeping well helps you to retain information better, so you're more likely to recall the answers when you see the test questions.

Getting good sleep means more than going to bed on time. It's important to allow your brain time to relax. Take study breaks from time to time so it doesn't get overworked, and don't study right before bed. Take time to rest your mind before trying to rest your body, or you may find it difficult to fall asleep.

Along with sleep, other aspects of physical health are important in preparing for a test. Good nutrition is vital for good brain function. Sugary foods and drinks may give a burst of energy but this burst is followed by a crash, both physically and emotionally. Instead, fuel your body with protein and vitamin-rich foods.

Also, drink plenty of water. Dehydration can lead to headaches and exhaustion, especially if your brain is already under stress from the rigors of the test. Particularly if your test is a long one, drink water during the breaks. And if possible, take an energy-boosting snack to eat between sections.

Along with sleep and diet, a third important part of physical health is exercise. Maintaining a steady workout schedule is helpful, but even taking 5-minute study breaks to walk can help get your blood pumping faster and clear your head. Exercise also releases endorphins, which contribute to a positive feeling and can help combat test anxiety.

When you nurture your physical health, you are also contributing to your mental health. If your body is healthy, your mind is much more likely to be healthy as well. So take time to rest, nourish your body with healthy food and water, and get moving as much as possible. Taking these physical steps will make you stronger and more able to take the mental steps necessary to overcome test anxiety.

Mental Steps for Beating Test Anxiety

Working on the mental side of test anxiety can be more challenging, but as with the physical side, there are clear steps you can take to overcome it. As mentioned earlier, test anxiety often stems from lack of preparation, so the obvious solution is to prepare for the test. Effective studying may be the most important weapon you have for beating test anxiety, but you can and should employ several other mental tools to combat fear.

First, boost your confidence by reminding yourself of past success—tests or projects that you aced. If you're putting as much effort into preparing for this test as you did for those, there's no reason you should expect to fail here. Work hard to prepare; then trust your preparation.

Second, surround yourself with encouraging people. It can be helpful to find a study group, but be sure that the people you're around will encourage a positive attitude. If you spend time with others who are anxious or cynical, this will only contribute to your own anxiety. Look for others who are motivated to study hard from a desire to succeed, not from a fear of failure.

Third, reward yourself. A test is physically and mentally tiring, even without anxiety, and it can be helpful to have something to look forward to. Plan an activity following the test, regardless of the outcome, such as going to a movie or getting ice cream.

When you are taking the test, if you find yourself beginning to feel anxious, remind yourself that you know the material. Visualize successfully completing the test. Then take a few deep, relaxing breaths and return to it. Work through the questions carefully but with confidence, knowing that you are capable of succeeding.

Developing a healthy mental approach to test taking will also aid in other areas of life. Test anxiety affects more than just the actual test—it can be damaging to your mental health and even contribute to depression. It's important to beat test anxiety before it becomes a problem for more than testing.

Study Strategy

Being prepared for the test is necessary to combat anxiety, but what does being prepared look like? You may study for hours on end and still not feel prepared. What you need is a strategy for test prep. The next few pages outline our recommended steps to help you plan out and conquer the challenge of preparation.

Step 1: Scope Out the Test

Learn everything you can about the format (multiple choice, essay, etc.) and what will be on the test. Gather any study materials, course outlines, or sample exams that may be available. Not only will this help you to prepare, but knowing what to expect can help to alleviate test anxiety.

Step 2: Map Out the Material

Look through the textbook or study guide and make note of how many chapters or sections it has. Then divide these over the time you have. For example, if a book has 15 chapters and you have five days to study, you need to cover three chapters each day. Even better, if you have the time, leave an extra day at the end for overall review after you have gone through the material in depth.

If time is limited, you may need to prioritize the material. Look through it and make note of which sections you think you already have a good grasp on, and which need review. While you are studying, skim quickly through the familiar sections and take more time on the challenging parts.

Write out your plan so you don't get lost as you go. Having a written plan also helps you feel more in control of the study, so anxiety is less likely to arise from feeling overwhelmed at the amount to cover.

Step 3: Gather Your Tools

Decide what study method works best for you. Do you prefer to highlight in the book as you study and then go back over the highlighted portions? Or do you type out notes of the important information? Or is it helpful to make flashcards that you can carry with you? Assemble the pens, index cards, highlighters, post-it notes, and any other materials you may need so you won't be distracted by getting up to find things while you study.

If you're having a hard time retaining the information or organizing your notes, experiment with different methods. For example, try color-coding by subject with colored pens, highlighters, or post-it notes. If you learn better by hearing, try recording yourself reading your notes so you can listen while in the car, working out, or simply sitting at your desk. Ask a friend to quiz you from your flashcards, or try teaching someone the material to solidify it in your mind.

Step 4: Create Your Environment

It's important to avoid distractions while you study. This includes both the obvious distractions like visitors and the subtle distractions like an uncomfortable chair (or a too-comfortable couch that makes you want to fall asleep). Set up the best study environment possible: good lighting and a comfortable work area. If background music helps you focus, you may want to turn it on, but otherwise keep the room quiet. If you are using a computer to take notes, be sure you don't have any other windows open, especially applications like social media, games, or anything else that could distract you. Silence your phone and turn off notifications. Be sure to keep water close by so you stay hydrated while you study (but avoid unhealthy drinks and snacks).

Also, take into account the best time of day to study. Are you freshest first thing in the morning? Try to set aside some time then to work through the material. Is your mind clearer in the afternoon or evening? Schedule your study session then. Another method is to study at the same time of day that you will take the test, so that your brain gets used to working on the material at that time and will be ready to focus at test time.

Step 5: Study!

Once you have done all the study preparation, it's time to settle into the actual studying. Sit down, take a few moments to settle your mind so you can focus, and begin to follow your study plan. Don't give in to distractions or let yourself procrastinate. This is your time to prepare so you'll be ready to fearlessly approach the test. Make the most of the time and stay focused.

Of course, you don't want to burn out. If you study too long you may find that you're not retaining the information very well. Take regular study breaks. For example, taking five minutes out of every hour to walk briskly, breathing deeply and swinging your arms, can help your mind stay fresh.

As you get to the end of each chapter or section, it's a good idea to do a quick review. Remind yourself of what you learned and work on any difficult parts. When you feel that you've mastered the material, move on to the next part. At the end of your study session, briefly skim through your notes again.

But while review is helpful, cramming last minute is NOT. If at all possible, work ahead so that you won't need to fit all your study into the last day. Cramming overloads your brain with more information than it can process and retain, and your tired mind may struggle to recall even previously learned information when it is overwhelmed with last-minute study. Also, the urgent nature of cramming and the stress placed on your brain contribute to anxiety. You'll be more likely to go to the test feeling unprepared and having trouble thinking clearly.

So don't cram, and don't stay up late before the test, even just to review your notes at a leisurely pace. Your brain needs rest more than it needs to go over the information again. In fact, plan to finish your studies by noon or early afternoon the day before the test. Give your brain the rest of the day to relax or focus on other things, and get a good night's sleep. Then you will be fresh for the test and better able to recall what you've studied.

Step 6: Take a Practice Test

Many courses offer sample tests, either online or in the study materials. This is an excellent resource to check whether you have mastered the material, as well as to prepare for the test format and environment.

Check the test format ahead of time: the number of questions, the type (multiple choice, free response, etc.), and the time limit. Then create a plan for working through them. For example, if you have 30 minutes to take a 60-question test, your limit is 30 seconds per question. Spend less time on the questions you know well so that you can take more time on the difficult ones.

If you have time to take several practice tests, take the first one open book, with no time limit. Work through the questions at your own pace and make sure you fully understand them. Gradually work up to taking a test under test conditions: sit at a desk with all study materials put away and set a timer. Pace yourself to make sure you finish the test with time to spare and go back to check your answers if you have time.

After each test, check your answers. On the questions you missed, be sure you understand why you missed them. Did you misread the question (tests can use tricky wording)? Did you forget the information? Or was it something you hadn't learned? Go back and study any shaky areas that the practice tests reveal.

Taking these tests not only helps with your grade, but also aids in combating test anxiety. If you're already used to the test conditions, you're less likely to worry about it, and working through tests until you're scoring well gives you a confidence boost. Go through the practice tests until you feel comfortable, and then you can go into the test knowing that you're ready for it.

Test Tips

On test day, you should be confident, knowing that you've prepared well and are ready to answer the questions. But aside from preparation, there are several test day strategies you can employ to maximize your performance.

First, as stated before, get a good night's sleep the night before the test (and for several nights before that, if possible). Go into the test with a fresh, alert mind rather than staying up late to study.

Try not to change too much about your normal routine on the day of the test. It's important to eat a nutritious breakfast, but if you normally don't eat breakfast at all, consider eating just a protein bar. If you're a coffee drinker, go ahead and have your normal coffee. Just make sure you time it so that the caffeine doesn't wear off right in the middle of your test. Avoid sugary beverages, and drink enough water to stay hydrated but not so much that you need a restroom break 10 minutes into the test. If your test isn't first thing in the morning, consider going for a walk or doing a light workout before the test to get your blood flowing.

Allow yourself enough time to get ready, and leave for the test with plenty of time to spare so you won't have the anxiety of scrambling to arrive in time. Another reason to be early is to select a good seat. It's helpful to sit away from doors and windows, which can be distracting. Find a good seat, get out your supplies, and settle your mind before the test begins.

When the test begins, start by going over the instructions carefully, even if you already know what to expect. Make sure you avoid any careless mistakes by following the directions.

Then begin working through the questions, pacing yourself as you've practiced. If you're not sure on an answer, don't spend too much time on it, and don't let it shake your confidence. Either skip it and come back later, or eliminate as many wrong answers as possible and guess among the remaining ones. Don't dwell on these questions as you continue—put them out of your mind and focus on what lies ahead.

Be sure to read all of the answer choices, even if you're sure the first one is the right answer. Sometimes you'll find a better one if you keep reading. But don't second-guess yourself if you do immediately know the answer. Your gut instinct is usually right. Don't let test anxiety rob you of the information you know.

If you have time at the end of the test (and if the test format allows), go back and review your answers. Be cautious about changing any, since your first instinct tends to be correct, but make sure you didn't misread any of the questions or accidentally mark the wrong answer choice. Look over any you skipped and make an educated guess.

At the end, leave the test feeling confident. You've done your best, so don't waste time worrying about your performance or wishing you could change anything. Instead, celebrate the successful completion of this test. And finally, use this test to learn how to deal with anxiety even better next time.

Review Video: Test Anxiety
Visit mometrix.com/academy and enter code: 100340

Important Qualification

Not all anxiety is created equal. If your test anxiety is causing major issues in your life beyond the classroom or testing center, or if you are experiencing troubling physical symptoms related to your anxiety, it may be a sign of a serious physiological or psychological condition. If this sounds like your situation, we strongly encourage you to seek professional help.

Online Resources

Due to our efforts to try to keep this book to a manageable length, we've created a link that will give you access to all of your online resources:

mometrix.com/resources719/staarg6rla

It's Your Moment, Let's Celebrate It!

Share your story @mometrixtestpreparation